W9-CNB-670

MAGNIFICENT WOMEN IN MUSIC

Magnificent Women in Music

by Heather Ball

Library and Archives Canada Cataloguing in Publication

Ball, Heather, 1978-
Magnificent women in music / by Heather Ball.

(Women's hall of fame series)
For children aged 9-13.
ISBN 1-897187-02-5

1. Women musicians--Juvenile literature. I. Title. II. Series.

ML3929.B187 2005   j780'.92'2   C2005-904201-X

Edited by Sandra Braun
Designed by Melissa Kaita

Printed and bound in Canada

Second Story Press gratefully acknowledges the support of the
Ontario Arts Council and the Canada Council for the Arts for our
publishing program. We acknowledge the financial support of
the Government of Canada through the Book Publishing Industry
Development Program.

Published by
SECOND STORY PRESS
20 Maud Street, Suite 401
Toronto, Ontario, Canada
M5V 2M5

www.secondstorypress.ca

TABLE OF CONTENTS

To my best friends
Megan and Erin

INTRODUCTION

In our lives, we all have challenges to face. One of the challenges I faced recently was writing this book. You may be wondering exactly what was so difficult — it's such a fun subject. So many women, for so many years, have been making incredible music that has made us think and touched our lives. Like me, you probably have lots of favorite songs, more than you can count. Maybe you listen to the same CD over and over again, or you purchase all of the mp3s you can find by your favorite artists? Thinking of my favorite women in music, I wondered how I could possibly choose just ten to write about.

The final decision was a big struggle; there are many, many more who deserve to be included here. In the end, I chose women who I think are not only great musicians, singers, songwriters and performers, but who had the courage to pursue their dreams despite some pretty difficult circumstances. Each one has a different story, much like every single person who will read this book. As you learn about their lives, I hope you see something of yourself, whether it's similar taste in music, a character trait such as persistence or bravery, or even something you hope to accomplish someday, such as writing your own song. While some of the women you're going to read about may not be on your playlist (some of them you may have never even heard of before picking up this book), I hope you feel inspired and entertained by their stories.

Although they all work in the same art form, their styles and lives are all very different. Clara Schumann was married with children and still managed to have a strong career as a concert pianist. Ethel Smyth was so determined to become a com-

poser that, at first, she accepted no money to have her music published, even though she deserved to be paid. Marian Anderson, who had one of the most beautiful singing voices in classical music, was rejected by the first music school she applied to. Ella Fitzgerald, as a Black woman in the first half of the twentieth century, faced a lot of discrimination, and was told she didn't deserve to be paid the same as white singers, even though her talent was huge. When she was a child, Buffy Sainte-Marie felt so estranged from her Aboriginal heritage that she felt she didn't fit in anywhere, and turned to music for comfort. Joni Mitchell is a great songwriter whose work is now studied in universities, but when she started out she had so little money she could hardly feed herself. In k.d. lang's hometown, people knew she was a bit strange, not really like anyone else, and that is a crucial reason why her music is appreciated today. It took a terrible accident and a broken jaw to help Chantal Kreviazuk realize that she wanted to write songs for the rest of her life. Measha Brueggergosman performs in spectacular costumes and has huge hair, because she embraces everything about herself that sets her apart from other people. Vanessa-Mae uses her mixed cultural background as inspiration to create music that is influenced by cultures all over the world.

It's hard to imagine what all these different women have in common, other than music, but there is one thing: hard work. From the time they realized that they wanted to dedicate their lives to music, each one worked very hard to keep her dreams alive. Whether it was something as simple as practicing endless scales on the piano, going to auditions or something as difficult as facing rejection — they all had hard times. But they didn't give up; they kept working.

What makes a person want to create music, despite how hard she must work to realize her dreams? Some people dream

Introduction

of performing in front of an audience who really understand their artistic vision. They imagine standing on a big stage in front of thousands of people who cheer and applaud. Some people have been blessed with unbelievable talent that they want to share with the rest of the world.

The biggest reason people make music isn't fame. Of course it can be glamorous and it's thrilling to be popular, but actually, being famous isn't the most important thing at all. If you asked these women, they would probably tell you that they make music because they love it. They love performing, they love practicing, they love creating art, they love sharing ideas, and they love communicating with the listeners and fans every time one of their songs is played. The old saying, "music is the universal language," is an old saying because it's true. Have you ever listened to a song written by someone you've never met before and felt like smiling, or crying, or jumping up and down? Have you ever heard a song and understood exactly what the singer was trying to communicate, because you'd gone through the same thing? Not many art forms have the power to affect our moods, or even our lives, in only a few short minutes.

If you admire gutsy women, and hope to grow and become one yourself, this book is for you. I hope you'll admire these magnificent women musicians as much as I do. Of course, you don't have to be a professional musician to read this book either. If you like singing by the campfire in the summer; dancing around your room to a great song; playing in the school band or a band with your friends; humming as you walk down the street; or even if you're trying to learn a new instrument, this book is for you. All you need is a love of music and the way it can enrich your life.

CLARA WIECK SCHUMANN

1819 – 1896

Even when a person is very talented and gifted, she may not have the self-esteem to realize her full potential. Clara Schumann started off as a shy little girl with no time for friends, because she was always practicing music. Up until she was a teenager, her strict father controlled every part of her life and made all of her decisions. He wanted Clara to have only music in her life, no family or relationships. But when Clara grew up and met her husband, she knew she wanted music and family. It took years of performing and hard work, and lots of courage to stand up to her father, but all the struggles helped Clara realize that she could rely on her abilities and brains to manage her own career, make her own money and support a family. By trusting

A young Clara seated with sheets of music on her lap. Clara's love for music began at at a very early age.

in herself, and by working hard to be the best musician and parent she could be, Clara transformed herself into a confident person—a celebrated pianist, composer and teacher.

Clara's parents were named Friedrich and Marianne. Friedrich was a well-respected music teacher who taught many students in the city of Leipzig, Germany. The piano store he owned was located in the downstairs part of their home. Marianne also taught music, and was a performer with a beautiful soprano voice. They met when Marianne hired Friedrich to give her singing lessons. Clara was born on September 13, 1819. She had two younger brothers named Alvin and Gustav.

Friedrich was ambitious and wanted to be known as the greatest piano teacher in Germany. From the time Clara was born, he dreamed of molding her into a famous pianist, thanks to his training. He constantly pushed his wife and children to practice and to be perfect musicians, and often went too far. Although the Wieck house was filled with the sounds of music, it was also filled with the sounds of Friedrich screaming at Marianne and the children. If someone did something he did not like,

such as play the wrong note during practice, his short temper got the better of him and he would yell at the top of his voice. After years of abuse, Marianne left when Clara was just five. It was the most difficult decision she'd ever had to make, because it meant that she would not only be left with nothing, but would also lose her children. At the time, it was the law that the father got custody of the children when a couple divorced.

Clara was a bit different from most children, because she didn't start talking until she was about four years old. Some scholars think that because there was so much noise in the house, she felt it best to keep quiet. For the first part of her life, people thought Clara was deaf and would never learn to talk, but Friedrich refused to believe that his own daughter could not hear or play music. If that were true, what would become of his dream of Clara as a famous pianist, of himself as a famous teacher? He ignored what others said and started teaching her to play the piano.

With Marianne gone, Friedrich focused almost all of his attention on Clara and her music lessons. It was obvious that Clara was not like his other students; she learned quickly and easily, as though she had been born with her fingers on the piano keys. It was hard to deal with her father's demands for perfection, but she loved playing so much that she practised for hours every day and always gave her best effort. She felt that the only way her father would love her would be if she played the piano better than anyone else.

When she was nine years old, Clara played in public for the first time, at a concert that featured several other musicians who were older than she was. Her father arranged every detail, from choosing Clara's dress, to deciding which pieces she would perform. Clara was nervous, because she was used to playing only for her father or a few of his friends, but she also couldn't wait to hear a crowd of people clapping just for her. After the performance, everyone in the audience agreed that Clara was

> The story of Clara Wieck Schumann and Robert Schumann has inspired two feature films, which are based on their lives. An American production, *Song of Love*, starring Katharine Hepburn, and a German production, *Spring Symphony* (*Fruehlingssinfonie*, in its original language), starring Nastassja Kinski.

a child prodigy, a *wunderkind*, with an astonishing talent.

The success of Clara's first concert encouraged Friedrich to make her practice even harder. You could always find her sitting at the piano, and on top of practising, she started composing her own music. Friedrich was proud of her, but instead of mainly praising his daughter's natural gifts, he took a lot of credit for himself—he was, after all, the teacher. Clara wasn't allowed to do normal activities like playing outside with other children, because it might interfere with her music training. She didn't even go to a regular school, but took lessons at home.

In 1830, Clara met the person who would change her life. Robert Schumann, a young man of 18, came to study music with Friedrich. He lived at the Wieck house and practiced for hours a day, just as Clara did. He had a lively personality and hated sitting still, so he sometimes found it hard to follow a strict practice schedule, but he admired Friedrich as a teacher and wanted nothing more than to be a great musician. He even composed his own music, which was something else he and Clara had in common.

Clara continued to perform in her home country, and soon her father decided she was ready to go on tour. In 1831, Fried-

In 1986, Clara was honored with her own postage stamp in Germany.

rich took his daughter and traveled to Paris, stopping in different cities along the way for Clara to give concerts. The audiences were all amazed that such a young child could play so expertly and over the next few years, Friedrich arranged for Clara to play as many concerts as possible.

Up until she became a teenager, Clara dedicated herself to obeying her father's wishes. But as she got older, she started to speak her mind and do things her own way. Of course her love of music was always the most important thing, but she wouldn't always listen to Friedrich when he ordered her around. Before, when he told her she wasn't doing a good job, she got upset and said nothing. But the more she played in public, and heard the audiences applauding her, the more she realized that it was her hard work and her hours of practice that had got her there, not her father's yelling. Instead of listening to his sharp words, Clara filled her head with the music of Chopin, Bach and Beethoven.

Robert Schumann continued to live in the Wieck house and Clara became his friend and biggest fan. Whenever he com-

In 1997, Clara was featured on the 100 DM (the Deutsche Mark was the German currency before the Euro) bill. The background is made up of buildings from historic Leipzig. The reverse side of the bill has a grand piano and the Hoch Conservatorium in Frankfurt where Clara taught for four years.

A portrait of Clara at the piano in 1835. Clara was 16 at the time.

posed a new piece, Clara wanted to be the first to learn it. When his music was published, Clara showed almost more excitement than he did. In turn, Robert was amazed by Clara's talent. He wasn't jealous that she played the piano better than he did, although she was younger, and he valued her opinion on his compositions. By the time she was a young woman of 16, Clara had fallen in love with Robert.

Right from the start, their relationship faced problems, especially from Friedrich. He wanted to control Clara's life forever, just as he always had. He didn't think Robert was good enough for his daughter and wouldn't let them see each other. Besides, he thought Clara's musical career would be over if she got married and started a family, and all his work would go to waste. But Friedrich couldn't watch them all the time, and secretly they sent each other notes and met when they could.

Clara Wieck Schumann

After a series of performances in Vienna, Austria, Clara was honored with the title of Royal and Imperial Virtuoso by the country's emperor. Every concert sold out as soon as tickets went on sale, and Clara was a big musical celebrity. The late nights of playing piano and the many performances left her exhausted, but finally she got the success she deserved. She wrote letters to Robert, telling him of her achievements.

Touring was the perfect situation to keep Clara and Robert apart, but they stayed in contact and their feelings for each other didn't change. In 1837, Robert asked Friedrich's permission to marry Clara (this was the tradition at the time), but of course he refused. The law was on his side, too, because it said that until Clara was 21, she was considered a child and needed her guardian's consent to get married. Frustrated, Clara and Robert sued Friedrich and the court battle lasted for one long year. Friedrich was so angry he refused to give in, would not speak to his daughter or give her any of the money she'd earned from the concerts he had arranged. In the end, the young couple won, and married in 1840, just one day before Clara's 21st birthday.

One promise Clara made to herself was that the new marriage would not interfere with her music, and it didn't. At the time, women didn't usually have families and careers at the same time, but Clara was the exception. Even when she became pregnant in 1841, she continued to perform, which was unusual because people thought pregnant women should stay home all the time. But Clara was too popular for anyone to care about what was usual. Over the years, she had seven more children.

The day after their wedding (Clara's birthday) Robert gave her a diary. He thought they should each keep it for one week and write back and forth to each other, which they did for many years. The diary still exists today to tell their story.

In 1844 Clara and Robert moved to Dresden. They gave music lessons, composed and performed as much as they could. Robert's fame as a composer grew, but Clara was always more famous and more confident about her abilities. She also earned more money than he did, which started to bother him. When he accepted a job as an orchestra conductor in Düsseldorf, Robert was very nervous and didn't know if he was good enough. Clara tried to encourage him, but he let his bad feelings get the best of him and didn't do well.

Robert suffered from serious depression and spent time in and out of psychiatric hospitals. With a family to watch over and a career to keep up, Clara had to be strong enough for both of them. She fretted over her husband's illness, but she knew that panicking wouldn't help, and kept up with her music. In 1856, Robert died in a psychiatric hospital, leaving Clara to take care of everything herself. To be sure there was enough money, Clara toured, performed, and was sometimes on the road for ten months out of the year.

If not for her work, family and friendships with other musicians, Clara would have found it much more difficult to get by as a single mother. While touring, she met people from all over the world and kept in touch with them by writing letters. She was especially good friends with Johannes Brahms, who met the Schumanns as a young man and went on to become a famous composer. Clara encouraged him to pursue his dream as she had, and critiqued his compositions to help make them better. She also used her influence in the music world to help him become recognized. In return, Johannes helped watch over the family when Robert was sick and gave his opinion on Clara's music when she asked for it.

In 1878 Clara gave a big performance in Leipzig, to celebrate the 50th anniversary of her career as a concert pianist. During the concert, she only played songs written by Robert and played better than she ever had. The members of the audience were so moved by the music and by their admiration for Clara, they stood up to applaud and threw flowers at her feet.

In her lifetime, Clara wrote 66 pieces of music, which might sound like a lot, but is a pretty modest number compared to what many composers of the time created. But most of these composers were men, who did not have to raise families by themselves and give lessons and tour all over Europe. Clara was never judged on the quantity of her work, but rather the quality of the pieces and was respected for her talent as a composer and performer.

Clara died of a stroke on May 20, 1896, in Frankfurt, Germany. She was surrounded by her family at home, and when she knew the time of her death was near, she asked her grandson Ferdinand to play one of the first pieces Robert ever composed, called *Papillons* (French for butterflies). It was the last music she heard.

Clara's career was one of the longest of any pianist of the 19th century, and she continued to perform until she was in her 70s. Scholars who have studied her believe she may have given as many as 1,500 performances in her lifetime. A great teacher, composer, and performer, Clara Schumann worked very hard to prove she did not have to choose between her career and her family. Although she started out with very little independence, Clara grew up to become a woman who took charge of her life and never let anything stop her from achieving her dreams.

DAME ETHEL SMYTH

1858 – 1944

From the time she was a child, Ethel Smyth hated waiting. One day, she was riding with her family in a carriage, which was moving uphill. Ethel wished the wheels would turn faster. Even with her short legs, she knew she could reach the top of the hill much faster if she just got out and walked. To her mother's surprise, Ethel jumped out of the carriage while it was moving and landed with a thump on her back, instead of on her feet. Everyone thought she was hurt, but she simply got up and dusted herself off. Ethel Smyth was never a person who was just along for the ride. She took her own road, and even if things went wrong, Ethel always got up and tried again.

Magnificent Women in Music

Before Ethel was born on April 23, 1858, her family lived in India. Her father was Major General J.H. Smyth, a successful army officer who worked in Bengal, India. He met Ethel's mother, Nina, in England in 1848. She was a very smart woman who spoke five languages and enjoyed singing and playing the piano.

The Smyth family was a large one—Ethel was the fourth child out of eight. With so many others around, it wasn't easy to get people to notice her, so Ethel developed a strong personality from the time she was a baby. If someone challenged her to a race, Ethel always said yes, determined to win. If someone climbed to a very high tree branch, Ethel had to climb even higher. Often, she misbehaved and did things that she knew would get her into trouble. But she didn't care, because she wanted to prove that she wasn't afraid of anything.

One day, a boy from school dared her to ride around on the back of a short black pig. Some children, like Ethel's sister Alice, would never dream of doing something so unladylike, but Ethel didn't think twice. She completely ruined the new white dress she was wearing, but it was so fun and entertaining to all who watched that Ethel didn't mind when she was later punished.

Ethel befriended many famous people, and one of her best friends was the writer Virginia Woolf. After reading *A Room of One's Own*, Ethel asked Virginia for advice on her own writing. The two women encouraged each other and exchanged hundreds of letters between 1930 and Virginia's death in 1941.

When Ethel did things of which her mother didn't approve, she had to go sit in the attic. It was a boring place, with no toys to play with and nobody to talk to. But Ethel knew how to get around the rules. Secretly, she took books up to the attic, so after awhile her punishments weren't so bad. Ethel's ability to take a bad situation and make it fun helped her a lot in her adult life, whether she found herself alone in a new place without friends, or even in prison! She always turned difficult experiences into positive ones.

Just like her mother, Ethel took piano lessons and sang very well. At first, the songs she practiced weren't very exciting, but she loved music so much that she kept up with her studies. She also had a governess who had studied at the Music Conservatory in Leipzig, Germany. The governess taught her new songs and introduced her to the music of Ludwig van Beethoven. Ethel couldn't believe that he wrote such beautiful music even though he was deaf and could only imagine the sound of a note.

Ethel decided that she wanted to be a composer, too. She took classes so she could learn how to take the music she heard in her head and write it down on paper. She also learned music theory, the study of the different elements of music, their importance, and how they relate to each other in a composition. Whenever she could, Ethel went to hear orchestras play in London and wished they were playing her music. With all her new knowledge, Ethel began to compose her own pieces.

Her father wasn't at all supportive of his daughter's dream and hoped it was just a phase. He thought the idea of Ethel becoming a composer was ridiculous. Most composers at the time were men, and besides, how could Ethel write music and have a husband at the same time? Everyone expected her to get married, raise children and forget about music. Her family even started planning her "coming out party," an event where Ethel was supposed to be introduced as a young woman to any men who might wish to marry her.

But the party never happened. Ethel was so set on becoming a composer that she told her father he had to let her go to school in Leipzig. He refused: it wasn't proper for a young lady to be in a big city by herself. Some people would just give up, but not Ethel. Instead she argued with him for two years until finally he agreed, and when Ethel was 19 she traveled to Germany to start her new life.

Magnificent Women in Music

Living on her own was easy for Ethel. She had waited to be independent her whole life and was eager to experience everything the city had to offer, especially its music. At first, she was warned by locals that she shouldn't go out by herself because it wasn't right for someone her age to go out unchaperoned. Ethel found a creative solution. She put on a plain dress, glasses, and a curly gray wig. To complete the old-woman disguise, Ethel spoke in a high, shaky voice. Nobody knew she was actually a young woman, and even a friend from school didn't recognize her.

Ethel expected a lot from the Leipzig Conservatory; after all, it was one of the best music schools in Europe. Because she was especially excited to meet other young composers, she was disappointed to find out that many students didn't share her goal. They wanted to become music teachers, not composers, and weren't interested in writing their own pieces. The teachers didn't encourage creativity, and Ethel's outgoing personality didn't match their traditional tastes. After one year, Ethel left the school to study privately with Heinrich von Herzogenberg, an Austrian composer. Heinrich introduced her to famous musicians like Clara Schumann, Peter Tschaikovsky and Johannes Brahms.

The more she studied, the more Ethel was inspired. She wrote some chamber music (music played by five or six musicians, meant to be performed in a small room), sonatas for string instruments like the cello and the violin and *lieder*, which are pieces that tell a story and are usually written for one singer and a piano.

Convinced that her music should be published, Ethel went to see Dr. Hase, the business manager of a music publishing company. Before he even heard Ethel's songs, he told her that women did not make good composers, and that nobody would be interested in anything written by a woman. He said that the few women who did compose, like Clara Schumann, were sim-

ply lucky and didn't make as much money as men. What he said bothered Ethel, but she insisted that he at least give her chance. After hearing Ethel's pieces, Dr. Hase agreed to publish them, but he wouldn't pay her anything. Ethel agreed, because she thought she had no choice. She always regretted not standing up for herself that day, and promised never to let anyone take advantage of her again.

> "I had a foreknowledge of the difficulties that, in a world arranged by man for man's convenience, beset the woman who leaves the traditional path to compete for bread and butter, honours and emoluments. The people who have helped me most at difficult moments of my musical career…have been members of my own sex."
> - Dame Ethel Smyth

Ethel's ambition grew, and she decided that instead of writing for small groups of instruments, she wanted to write for orchestras. She studied how to make so many musical lines fit together and wrote *Serenade*, which was made up of four movements (sections) and an overture at the beginning. In 1890, it was performed in London at the Crystal Palace and the reviewers praised Ethel's talents. Her hard work was starting to pay off. Inspired by *Serenade*'s success, Ethel spent the next year composing orchestra music. She called her creation *Mass in D* and put all her passion into the striking music. It was performed in London, England, at the Royal Albert Hall in January 1893. Although the audience who attended the performance clapped loudly, the newspaper reviews weren't positive. But Ethel had come too far and worked too hard to give up. She decided to take a new direction.

Ethel thought seriously about what kind of music she really wanted to write. She loved orchestras, dramatic music and storytelling. Encouraged by Hermann Levi, a famous German conductor, Ethel started to write her first opera called *Fantasio*. Her friend Henry Brewster, a writer from the United States,

"The whole English attitude towards women in fields of art is ludicrous and uncivilized. There is no sex in art. How you play the violin, paint, or compose is what matters."
- Dame Ethel Smyth, *Streaks of Life*

helped write the lyrics in German, and the opera debuted in Weimar, Germany, because operas were not very popular in London at the time. The critics praised *Fantasio* for its rich music, but the reviews didn't consider it a hit show.

With each project, Ethel tried to learn something and to improve her abilities. In 1902, her second opera *Der Wald* (The Forest) played in Berlin and London. The work made history on March 11, 1903, when it was performed at New York's Metropolitan Opera House. It was the first opera composed by a woman to be shown on the famous stage. After the first show, the audience gave Ethel a ten-minute-long standing ovation.

Ethel showed the best of her talents with her most famous opera, *The Wreckers*. The first version of the libretto was written by Henry in French, and later translated into German and English. It tells the story of a small village in Cornwall on the coast of England. The villagers refuse to keep the light burning in the lighthouse, causing shipwrecks. After the ships crash, the village people steal the loot on the boat. The opera's main character, Thirza, tries to stop them.

The struggles Ethel faced as a woman in the music world inspired her to join another cause: the suffragist movement, to give women the right to vote in elections. Only men were allowed to vote at the time and Ethel knew that keeping half the population out of making important decisions was unfair. One of her good friends, Emmeline Pankhurst, founded a group called the Women's Social and Political Union (W.S.P.U.). Just like Ethel, Emmeline was an outgoing, passionate person who never gave up even when something seemed impossible. Using her musical talent, Ethel did her part to help the W.S.P.U. She wrote the group's anthem, called "The March of the Women," which also became a theme song for feminists in England. They sang it at meetings, rallies and while walking down the street to spread their message of equality. The suffragists were frustrated with the government, who didn't take them seriously. In 1912, the group marched along Downing Street in London, but they got carried away and started throwing rocks. One rock that Ethel threw broke the window of the colonial secretary, an important person in government. Because of their protest, 150 women were arrested and sent to jail.

Her sentence was for two months, but Ethel was happy to be released after only a few weeks. For someone who loved her freedom, spending most of the day locked up was hard to deal with. But her creative mind kept her spirits high. She led the other prisoners in singing "The March of the Women," and kept the beat by tapping her toothbrush against the iron bars of her cell.

Once free, Ethel moved away from England to Cairo, Egypt, and began again to compose operas. For the first time, Ethel began with lyrics written in English and created *The Boatswain's Mate*, a comedy. Her main character, Mrs. Waters, is a strong woman who runs an inn, and proves she is no fool when a man tries to trick her.

In 1922, for her contributions to British music and culture, Ethel was honored with the title Dame Commander of the Order of the British Empire, which is given to exceptional citizens. She also received an honorary degree in music from Oxford University (a degree given to someone who has not attended the school, but who is honored for their life's accomplishments) for the great body of work she created.

Throughout the 1920s and 1930s, Ethel continued to compose music. She wrote two more operas, *Fête Galante* in 1922 and *Entente Cordiale* in 1925. She acted as if nothing was wrong, but all the while she kept a secret. At around the age

of 55, Ethel noticed a ringing sound in her ears that wouldn't go away. At first she didn't think much of it, but as the years passed, Ethel knew she was losing her hearing. She knew that if she went completely deaf, her music career would come to an end, but she kept composing as long as she could, even if sometimes she had to strain to hear the notes. Her last work was *The Prison* written, in 1930. Performed by an orchestra and singers, the work was based on the writing of Ethel's friend Henry Brewster, who had died in 1908.

When Ethel could no longer hear, she didn't decide to live a quiet life. Instead, she began a new, successful career as a writer. She wrote ten books, mostly telling the story of her life, her impressions of music and of the famous people she'd met over the years. People liked Ethel's books because her writing style was funny, and reading them was like sitting next to Ethel, talking with a friend.

The year Ethel turned 75, her music was performed all over London as a tribute to a lifetime of accomplishments. By that time, she couldn't hear the music, but it was thrilling to be the guest of honor and to sit next to the Queen of England during concerts. On May 8, 1944, Ethel died at her home in Surrey, England. She had faced many obstacles over the years, but sexist attitudes and criticism never dragged her down. One of the most passionate composers of her time, a feminist and writer, Ethel proved that with perseverance, you can do anything.

MARIAN ANDERSON

1897 – 1993

Marian Anderson couldn't concentrate in her grade one class. It wasn't that the lessons were boring, or that she had trouble understanding; it was because the music room was right next door. All day long, through the wall, she heard the sounds of the piano playing and children singing. Even though Marian was only six years old at the time, she knew she wanted her life to be like one big music class, so she could sing all day long.

Born in Philadelphia, Pennsylvania, on February 27, 1897, Marian was known around her neighborhood as the girl with the huge, rich voice. Young girls often have very high singing voices, but Marian's was deep and low. When she sang, her

voice filled a room. She loved singing so much that she was a member of both the junior and the senior choirs at the Union Baptist Church. Her range (how many notes she could reach) was so big that although her voice was naturally contralto, she could sing almost any part.

John Anderson, her father, worked for a market, delivering ice and coal. He always walked tall and proud, especially on Sundays when he was the head usher at church. Her mother, Anna, raised Marian and her two sisters, Alyce and Ethel, and taught them to work hard at everything they did.

Life wasn't easy for most Black people at the time, because racism was everywhere. In fact, slavery was still legal in the United States up until 1865, not long before Marian's birth. Black slaves were considered the property of white landowners and forced to work all day, every day, and had no freedom of their own. The racist attitudes of slavery still existed in many people's minds as Marian grew up. It sounds ridiculous to us today, but at the time, people were often judged by the color of their skin, not by how good a person they were, how kind, smart or talented. Segregation was everywhere, too, especially in the southern United States, which means that Black people couldn't attend the same churches, go to the same schools or even drink from the same water fountains as white people. It was hard for them to get an education or a job, no matter how smart they were, simply based on the fact that they were Black. Marian learned very quickly that to be successful, she would have to work extra hard and be extra determined to pursue her dreams.

On the day her father brought home a piano, Marian was thrilled.

> Some books about Marian Anderson might give her a different birthday than this book. Throughout Marian's lifetime, she always said her birthday was February 17, 1902. But after her death, her official birth certificate was found, which showed the real date as February 27, 1897.

Marian Anderson

She'd spent so many hours, sitting at a table pretending it was a piano, moving her fingers as if she were playing. There was no money for lessons, but with the help of a few books that explained the notes and what keys to play, Marian learned to play music and sing at the same time. Her favorite songs were gospel or spiritual songs, like the ones she sang at church.

Marian's father died when she was just 12, and because the Anderson women didn't have any money, they moved in with their grandparents. Life was less relaxed in the new house, because Marian's grandparents were strict, and Anna wasn't around as much as before. She took a job cleaning department stores to earn money to support the family.

Marian also did her part to help out. By the time she was in high school, she was getting paid to sing at churches and give small performances around the city, making a couple of dollars per show. Word of her spectacular talent spread, until it reached a famous tenor, Roland Hayes, who came to perform as a guest soloist at Marian's church. Roland was a Black man with a successful career as a singer. He could sing in French, German and Italian, each one as if it were his first language. Because the congregation was so proud of her, Marian was asked to perform at the same concert as Roland.

The second Marian began to sing, Roland knew she had a great gift. Afraid it would go to waste without proper training, he encouraged her family to let her study with his teacher in Boston. Marian's grandmother would hear nothing of it. She didn't want her granddaughter to leave home at such a young age. Marian was disappointed, but there was nothing she could do.

As it turned out, Marian didn't have to go far to find another teacher. She studied with a local woman named Mary Patterson. Before taking lessons, Marian had never really thought about how she sang, she just did it. With Mary, she began to learn about the proper breathing techniques, how to open her

mouth wide to let all the sound come out and how to sing without hurting her voice. But Marian progressed so quickly that soon Mary had nothing else to teach her, and a new teacher, Agnes Reifsnyder, took over.

Marian considered attending the music school in Philadelphia and she went across town to inquire. There were other girls there, and a puzzled Marian watched as the school receptionist helped each one of them before her. When she finally got her turn, she was told that the school didn't take "colored" people. Marian hadn't noticed it at first, but the other girls in the line were white and she was the only Black person there. She was told to leave. Marian knew she was a better singer than most of the girls at the school that day; why wouldn't they give her a chance?

Although Marian knew white people didn't always accept Black people, she hadn't thought that segregation would keep her from studying music. She believed in herself and in her singing voice. At many concert halls, if Black people were allowed in at all, they could only sit in the very back rows. Marian dreamed about the day when a Black person could sit wherever she wanted.

But there were people who recognized the great talent in Marian and would not pass up the chance to help her. Giuseppe Boghetti was a famous Italian voice teacher. He was stern and wouldn't accept anything less than the best. On the day in 1920 when Marian went to audition to be his pupil, he told her that he didn't have time to take new students. But he listened anyway, and after Marian finished singing, he said "I'll make room for you right away." Under his direction, Giuseppe promised, Marian would become a world-class singer. Not only did he teach her more technique, but he taught her about classical music and opera.

In 1923, Marian entered and won a singing contest held by the Philadelphia Philharmonic. She was the first Black person

ever to do so. Marian also began traveling around to perform, working with an accompanist, Billy King. Soon, she was earning up to one hundred dollars for just one concert. She saved that money and bought a house for her mother and sisters, right across the street from her grandparents.

As much as she tried, Marian didn't succeed every time. In April of 1925, she was scheduled to give a big concert in New York, to a mostly white audience. She would be singing very difficult pieces, and still hadn't mastered singing in different languages, the way Roland Hayes had. When she got onstage, she was devastated to see only a very small audience. She tried to be brave, and performed anyway, but at the end there was hardly any applause. The article that appeared in the newspaper the next day said that Marian's performance was stiff and without feeling.

More determined than ever to prove herself as a singer, Marian booked passage on a ship to London, England, in October 1927. It was hard to find the money for the trip, but with her savings and a small scholarship from the National Association of Negro Musicians, she was able to go. She knew that some of the most respected teachers were in Europe and that if she was going to improve, she had to work with the best. She studied with many famous instructors, including Master Raimund von Zur Muhlen and Roger Quilter, but because she wasn't making much money, she had to go back to the United States.

Back at home, Marian was restless. Although she enjoyed performing locally, she needed the challenge of learning to sing in foreign languages; how would she be able to do that when all she spoke was English? She saved all the money she could and left for Germany, where she could immerse herself in classical music and

In January, 2005, the United States Postal Service issued a stamp in honor of Marian Anderson. The picture on the stamp was painted by a Canadian, Albert Slark, of Ajax, Ontario.

A portrait of Marian Anderson singing in 1940.

learn the language. If she understood the words to every song she sang, the emotion was sure to come through.

Rulle Rasmussen, a music promoter, and Kosti Vehanen, a talented piano accompanist, were well known in the European music world. They met Marian in Berlin and immediately offered her a tour of Norway and Finland, a total of six concerts. Marian agreed, trying not to show how excited she was, and set out on the tour, during which every show sold out.

With a new confidence and a better understanding of the emotion behind music, Marian's voice was better than ever. The audiences responded as enthusiastically as if they were the congregation at the Union Baptist Church in Philadelphia. She sang in England, France, Italy, Russia, Austria and Switzerland. People in Europe were different from those in the United States. They only cared that she was an incredible singer, not that she was a Black woman. Arturo Toscanini, one of the best orchestra conductors of the time, said to Marian: "Yours is a voice such as one hears once in a hundred years."

Having made it in Europe, Marian still felt she had something to prove in America. In 1935, she was scheduled to per-

form a big concert at the New York Town Hall and had chosen a very difficult piece as her first song. It was written by Handel and opened with a note that lasted 30 seconds. She also sang a spiritual song called "The Crucifixion." At the end, the applause was like thunder. The following day, the *New York Times* wrote that Marian was "one of the great singers of our time." She had conquered the music world of America and in 1936, even performed for President Roosevelt at the White House. He and his wife Eleanor were big fans of Marian's and spoke out openly against racism. They continued to support Marian throughout her career.

With all the success at home and abroad, Marian sometimes forgot about the racism that had almost held her back so many years before. But in certain parts of the States, there was still a strong separation between Black people and white people. Marian fought against it. Whenever she gave a concert at a segregated venue, she insisted that Black people be able to sit in any seat or she would not perform.

Marian's fame grew until audiences of all colors wanted to see her perform. She wanted to put on a concert in Washington DC, and her manager began searching for a venue (a place for the concert) that would hold a few thousand people; by 1939, anywhere with only a few hundred seats was simply not big enough. DC's Daughters of the American Revolution (or DAR) Constitution Hall was perfect, except for one thing: only white artists could perform there. Marian Anderson—one of the world's best singers—was banned from performing in the country's capital because she was Black.

Not only were Marian's fans outraged, but so was anyone who cared about civil rights (or rights of citizens). Many politicians, including President Roosevelt and his wife Eleanor, spoke out against the discrimination. Eleanor was even a member of DAR, and when other members refused to let Marian perform, she resigned in protest. Still, the rule was not changed. Mar-

ian decided that if she could not perform at DAR's Constitution Hall, she would simply find another venue in Washington DC. The performance turned out to be one of the biggest of her career.

The Lincoln Memorial in Washington DC represents freedom and equality for all people, so when the U.S.'s secretary of the interior, Harold Ickes, asked Marian to perform there, she knew the event would be incredibly meaningful. The building has tall columns like a Greek temple and holds a statue of Abraham Lincoln. The day of the concert, Easter Sunday, 70,000 people gathered to hear Marian Anderson. Her voice was also broadcast to thousands more over the radio. Although she claims she was nervous and scared, you could not tell. Marian sang more proudly than ever before "Ave Maria," "My Soul Is Anchored in the Lord" and "America/My Country 'Tis of Thee."

Marian's ears rang with applause for several days afterward, but that achievement alone didn't mean the end of racism. Over the next several years, she continued touring back and forth between Europe and the United States. Traveling through parts of the southern United States, it was often hard to get a hotel room or even find a restaurant that would serve her dinner, even though she was one of the world's best singers. Marian never lost her cool or yelled, she simply went to the next restaurant, and the next, until she found one that would serve her. She would not give ignorant people the satisfaction of knowing they had hurt her, and she made a point of carrying herself with more dignity than anyone. Her strong, proud presence was what made her perfect for the next challenge.

> "No matter how big a nation is, it is no stronger that its weakest people, and as long as you keep a person down, some part of you has to be down there to hold him down, so it means you cannot soar as you might otherwise."
> - Marian Anderson

Marian Anderson

When opera fans heard that Marian had signed a contract to perform at the New York Metropolitan Opera, they were thrilled, but agreed it was long-overdue moment. Up until that point, because of racism and prejudice, no Black woman had ever performed on the Met's stage. In 1955, Marian became the first Black woman to do so, in the role of Ulrica, a fortune teller in the opera *Un ballo in maschera* (A Masked Ball) by Giuseppe Verdi. When *The New York Times* heard about the historic event, their reporter wrote: "Whenever there was discrimination against Miss Anderson the real suffering was not hers but ours. It was we who were impoverished, not she." Marian fell into the role with ease, even though she'd never worked as an actress before. She wore her hair loosely around her shoulders, instead of having it pinned back as usual, and she wore a long cape and flowing skirt for her costume. All who saw her performance were moved and agreed she was born for the opera. Her accomplishment helped to pave the way for a new generation of Black women opera singers, such as Leontyne Price, Jessye Norman, Barbara Hendricks and Grace Bumbry, to name only a few.

In the later years of her career, Marian used the time in between performances to work as a delegate to the United Nations. In 1957 she went on a goodwill tour, visiting Korea, India, Vietnam, India and Pakistan. For her work representing the Black community, President Kennedy's government awarded Marian the Presidential Medal of Freedom in 1963.

Her final concert was at Carnegie Hall in 1965. Although nobody wanted to think of a time when Marian would stop performing, she felt that a 40-year career was long enough—she had given over 1,000 performances, after all. She was also presented with several honorary degrees and received a Grammy Award for Lifetime Achievement in 1991. Marian spent most of her retirement years on her farm, Marianna (a combination of her name and her mother's name) in Connecticut. She cherished this peaceful time in her life, exploring the many acres of the farm and spending time with her family. She passed away in 1993.

Marian Anderson achieved her dream of singing all day long, but also accomplished more than she imagined she would. She helped change the music world, proving that talent and hard work are more important than what a person looks like or where they come from. She rose up from the racism and segregation that she experienced as a young person and refused to let prejudice keep her from having the career she always dreamed of. By the end of her years she had seen the end of segregation and the establishment of equal rights as a part of the law for people of all races. She got to see Black women excel not only in music, but in all sorts of areas, and she played a special part in making that happen. Her voice brought people together; it changed racist attitudes and broke down barriers. With a unique talent, dignity and pride, Marian made the world her stage.

ELLA FITZGERALD

1918 – 1996

Not everyone knows what they want to do with their lives right away. It can take time to discover what you love and what you're good at. Or, even if a person shows a talent for one thing, they may discover almost by accident that they were meant to go in a different direction. Even though Ella Fitzgerald loved to sing, she didn't know she could get up on a stage and do it for a living. But one day, a case of nerves made her unable to dance, and one of the best jazz performers of all time helped her begin her career.

On April 25, 1918, Ella Jane Fitzgerald was born. She spent the first few years of her life in the town of Newport News, Virginia, with her father William and her mother Temperance

Magnificent Women in Music

(Tempie, for short). Her parents divorced when Ella was very young and she moved with Tempie to Yonkers, New York.

In Yonkers, Tempie got married a second time, to a man named Joseph Da Silva. Their family grew, and soon Ella had a baby sister, Frances, in 1923. They didn't have a lot of money, and everyone pitched in, working as much as they could to pay for food and shelter. Joseph worked two jobs; as a ditch digger and as a chauffeur. Tempie also worked two jobs: she washed piles of clothes in a local laundromat, and worked as a caterer, preparing food for parties. Ella did her part too, running errands for people in the neighborhood.

When they found themselves with a bit of extra money, Ella's family bought records to play on their gramophone, which is an old-style record player. Her favorite singers were Mamie Smith and Ethel Waters. When she didn't feel like listening to a record, there was always something on the radio, and Ella always enjoyed popular music the most. She could learn the words quickly and sing along.

Ella and her friends loved learning the steps to the latest dance crazes, like the Suzy-Q and the Snake Hip. Other times, all the children in the neighborhood would get together and organize a baseball game. Ella was very good at sports and enjoyed hitting the ball as far as she could, then running around the bases, trying to be faster than anyone.

In school, Ella earned high marks and was very involved in extracurricular activities. She was a member of the glee club, or choir, and loved performing in school plays. The audience loved it when Ella tried to imitate one of her idols, Louis Armstrong, and sing in a low growl. Every student had to choose between taking art classes or music classes and for Ella, the

decision was easy. She couldn't draw, but she was becoming a better singer every day.

For a treat, Ella sometimes got to go to the Apollo Theater in nearby Harlem, to watch the singers and the bands perform. She dreamed about how great it would feel if one day, she could get on that very stage and sing her heart out. She never thought it would actually happen.

In 1932, when Ella was only 15 years old, Tempie died very suddenly. Ella lost interest in everything that used to be fun. She didn't want to sing, dance or play with her friends. But she remembered how her mother was such a strong person and worked so hard to give her daughters a good life. Ella knew she had to keep going, and build on everything Tempie did for her.

Amateur nights (when people who were not professional performers were allowed to go onstage and compete for prize money) were popular when Ella was a teenager, and she decided to enter one at the Harlem Apollo Theater, as a dancer. Before she went on, Ella wished she could back out—her legs turned to water and it felt like her stomach had a million butterflies in it. Once in front of the crowd, Ella was frozen on the spot. Everyone waited for her to begin, and she knew she had to do something. Instead of dancing, Ella began to sing. The band joined in her song and the audience cheered. Ella won the contest, a grand prize of $25.

The enthusiasm for Ella's unexpected singing was more than she expected. Whenever there was a talent contest, she entered it. She started talking to local musicians to find out how they got into the music business, and got the chance to audition for Chick Webb, who was a drummer and the leader of his own band. Ella began touring with him, singing with Charlie Linton, and making her own money as a performer.

In the late 1930s, jazz was becoming very popular, especially its early form called bebop. Ella always had the ability to figure out the latest trends and do them herself, and she

began singing bebop music with great success. The crowds liked her even more, because she didn't just sing, she would make her voice sound like trumpet or a saxophone in the band, or she would scat. Scatting is when the singer invents complicated melodies to go along with the music, and instead of using real words, uses different syllables.

No one could have guessed that a simple nursery rhyme could become a hit song, but Ella made it happen in 1938. She recorded the song "A-Tisket, A-Tasket," which sold thousands of copies, and Ella became famous almost overnight. Despite

all the attention, she tried not to let it go to her head. She remembered what Chick Webb told her, that when you rise up too fast, you can fall down even faster. Ella never took her success for granted.

Chick died of pneumonia in 1939 and the band picked Ella to be their new leader. It was scary for her; she wasn't used to being the main focus onstage all the time. At age 21, Ella was one of the youngest bandleaders of the time and what made the challenge even greater

Ella Fitzgerald in 1940.

was that she was a woman when most bandleaders were men. But she thought about all she had learned and soon Ella and Her Famous Orchestra continued touring where Chick had left off. Ella's newly-famous name helped the Orchestra attract big crowds and they played in theaters on Broadway in New York and in fancy hotels. It was an important time, as they were often the very first Black group to play at such places.

Trends come and go, and the time came, in the early 1940s, when big band music was no longer as popular. Ella left the group to perform as a solo singer, and went back to her favorite kind of music: jazz. Sometimes, she performed two concerts in one day, in completely different cities. With her talent for scat and bebop, she began touring with the great trumpet player Dizzy Gillespie. She recorded two songs that are now considered jazz classics, "Oh Lady Be Good" and "How High the Moon." Not only was Ella known for her jazz, but she also became famous for her soulful ballads. That type of song was very popular during World War II, when many young people fought overseas.

Ella met Ray Brown, a jazz bass player, and decided to marry him in 1948. They adopted a boy, whom they named Ray Junior, but the marriage didn't last and they divorced after about five years. It was a friendly separation; they continued to perform together and stayed friends.

Ray's manager, Norman Granz, was convinced that Ella could become a jazz superstar and he asked her to join his tour, Jazz at the Philharmonic. They did encounter problems while touring, especially when they played in cities where segregation existed, which means that Black people and white people, even though they lived in the same town, were very separate in many ways. Black people weren't allowed to sit in the front seats of public buses and some restaurants refused to serve them food. Black people had to use separate washrooms, or if they wanted to enter a building, they had to do so by a separate door. These

Magnificent Women in Music

Ella won 13 Grammy Awards for her music over her lifetime and for 18 years in a row was named the top female jazz singer by *Down Beat Magazine*.

terrible attitudes existed in the world of music, too. In segregated concert halls, Black members of the audience sat on one side and whites on the other. Some places did not even let Black musicians perform, no matter how famous they were. Or, if they did perform, the concert hall manager tried to cheat the performers by paying them half of what white musicians were paid.

Of course, many white people believed these things were wrong and fought to change attitudes. Norman was a white person who hated racism. It made him sick to see how many of the talented musicians he worked with were treated so poorly, just because they were Black. When he toured, Norman always insisted that Black musicians had to get paid the same as white musicians, and if the concert hall manager refused, they left. But sometimes problems arose that Norman couldn't prevent. One story says that Ella and the band were arrested backstage after performing in a segregated town, because of complaints from white citizens. Ella thought it was a ridiculous situation, but it became unbelievable when she got to the jail, and a police officer asked for her autograph.

All in all, it was an exciting time. The tour took Ella to places she had never been before, such as Europe and Japan. Because the audiences always went crazy when Ella performed, Norman decided he had to be her manager, and work especially hard on her solo career instead of simply having her along with the band. She put her confidence in him and signed on to his record label, Verve, as its very first singer. He worked hard to show the world what a great talent she had, and soon Ella was singing on television variety shows, which included music, dancing and skits. These shows were hosted by some of the biggest names in

music, such as Bing Crosby, Nat King Cole, and Dean Martin.

Another way Norman helped Ella's career was when he encouraged her to record an entire album of show tunes from famous Broadway shows, written by the composer Cole Porter. Creating the album meant taking a big chance, because originally, white artists performed many of the songs. *The Cole Porter Songbook* was a huge success and just the beginning of a series of songbooks Ella went on to record. Other songwriters to whom she paid tribute were Duke Ellington, Jerome Kern, and George and Ira Gershwin. After hearing the recording, Ira Gershwin said his songs sounded even better when Ella sang them. Today, the albums are considered classic recordings, a kind of encyclopedia of American music from the 1950s.

In the 1960s, more and more people started listening to rock 'n' roll music, and jazz wasn't quite so in demand any more. Ella moved to Beverly Hills, California, and took a break so she could spend time with Ray Junior. But the world missed Ella's singing. After a few years, she was invited to perform at jazz festivals and clubs across the United States. She kept on singing as long as she could.

For many years of her life, Ella battled diabetes, a disease where the body does not produce or properly use enough of the hormone insulin. It makes a person's blood sugar levels rise very high. Her family tried to convince her to stop performing, but Ella pushed herself for her love of music. Singing made her forget that she didn't feel

> Many celebrities were fans of Ella's music, especially the actress Marilyn Monroe. One story says that Marilyn called the owner of a Hollywood nightclub, the Mocambo, and requested that he book Ella to perform. If Ella sang there, Marilyn promised to attend every show, so that the nightclub would get a lot of publicity—and that's just what happened. Ella said later she was grateful to Marilyn for her encouragement.

45

her best. When she was onstage, the audience couldn't even tell that she was sick; she put all her energy into the show. Finally, she did have to stop performing when she was in her late sixties, because she needed medication and became tired very easily. When she retired, she had recorded about 200 albums.

Ella was awarded the National Medal for the Arts in 1987, just one in a string of awards she received. Both Yale and Dartmouth Universities presented her with honorary degrees, which were very special to her because she had never finished school. The Lincoln Centre Medallion was only given to classical singers and musicians, until Ella became the first jazz performer to receive it. She was the first woman to be awarded with the Whitney M. Young Jr. Award, given to someone who helps break down the barriers of racism and improve life for African-Americans.

During her career, Ella performed at New York's Carnegie Hall 26 times. For her 75th birthday, she was honored there with a huge party and ceremony, where celebrities from all parts of the music industry paid tribute to her life and career. Ella had gained fans all over the world, even in Italy where they affectionately called her "Mama Jazz." Ella joked that the name was fine by her, as long as they didn't call her "Grandma Jazz."

Ella passed away in 1996, but is as popular today as she was when she first began to sing. Her journey, from little girl with a big dream to international singing star, took her to places she never thought she'd go. It was not just the other cities and countries that made her journey worthwhile, but the fact that she experienced the racism of a segregated society, when even a talented singer was discriminated against, and lived to see a time when that was no longer tolerated. By insisting that she be treated fairly and by refusing to let racism get her down, Ella proved that the color of a person's skin has nothing to do with what she can accomplish. Nothing stood in the way of her com-

mitment to music and when asked what, to her, was better than singing, Ella's reply shows her complete devotion to her work: "The only thing better than singing is more singing." It is no wonder she is known as the "first lady of jazz."

BUFFY SAINTE-MARIE

1941 –

Because we are all different from one another, we all have our own unique ways of communicating. Some are excellent speakers and can stand up in front of a crowd. Some need to write their feelings down before sharing them. Others use their actions to demonstrate what they feel inside. You can also communicate through art, because there are so many different kinds to try, such as music, poetry, painting or sculpture. Buffy Sainte-Marie expresses herself in all of these ways and shares what she thinks about all kinds of issues, from Aboriginal rights to the environment. Even though she didn't get a lot of encouragement when she was a child, she learned to believe in herself and in the power of creativity.

Magnificent Women in Music

Buffy was born into the Cree Aboriginal community on a small reserve—the Piapot Reserve—near Regina, Saskatchewan. When she was just a baby, Buffy was orphaned when her mother died in a car crash. Her mother's family didn't have much money and wasn't able to care for her, and Buffy was adopted by an American family. Her adoptive parents were part Aboriginal, from the Micmac community, and they lived in the United States, first in Maine and later on in Massachusetts.

Growing up, Buffy didn't have much connection to her Aboriginal roots. She often wondered about her birth mother and the relatives she never knew. Each Aboriginal community is unique with different traditions and beliefs, and Buffy wished to be more in touch with her Cree heritage. She felt out of place in her adoptive home, and felt they didn't teach her about their Aboriginal background, but lived much in the same way as white people. There was something missing and it took a long time before she could fill the huge hole in her life.

It wasn't until Buffy was a teenager that she was able to find out about her birth family. Buffy was reunited with her Cree relatives. Even though she'd never met any of that part of her family before, they welcomed her warmly and Buffy felt she had come home for the first time. Suddenly, she understood that she had a place in the world, and all the questions she grew up with were answered.

Like a lot of musicians, Buffy started off on the piano when she was little. Music came naturally to her. She never learned to read the notes on the page, and instead played everything by ear. She had tons of ideas for songs swimming around in her head. In high school she started playing the guitar and right away began experimenting with ways to change the sound. The piano is always tuned the same way, but a guitar's strings can be tightened or loosened to make chords (a combination of notes played at the same time) that sound different from traditional chords. Buffy also liked the guitar because all she had to do was put it over her shoulder and carry it anywhere she felt like playing.

Buffy Sainte-Marie

One kind of place Buffy brought her guitar was to the local coffeehouse when she was a student at the Univer-

sity of Massachusetts. Buffy loved it there, among other young people who sat together for hours, talking and sharing ideas. Music wasn't something she imagined doing as a career, because she was studying to become a teacher. But it felt good to share her songs with other people. Before that time, Buffy didn't play in front of others, because she didn't think she was good enough. At university, when she lived in the dorm, she met Theresa de Kerpely, a writer who supported her creative talents. At the coffeehouse, Buffy earned about five dollars a night, singing songs she had written like "Now that the Buffalo's Gone" and "Ananias." Many of Buffy's songs were protest songs, where the lyrics speak out against things like war and injustice.

By 1963, the name Buffy Sainte-Marie was quite famous among people who listened to folk music. The main part of the music scene was in Greenwich Village, New York City, which was known as a place where many artists, writers and musicians lived. Buffy's voice is very unique and high. The pitch goes up and down in waves. It's very influenced by her Aboriginal roots—their legends say that Native People were taught to sing by eagles. Buffy kept experimenting with her sound and learned to play the mouth bow, a traditional instrument of the Aboriginal People. It looks a lot like a bow you could use with an arrow. It is made of a long piece of curved wood with tiny holes on each end. A piece of wire is stretched between both ends and it is played with the mouth.

Buffy recorded her first album in 1964, called I*t's My Way.* She was only 23 years old, but her talent as a musician and a political poet showed she was smarter than many people her age. It was Buffy's first time recording anything, and she just played each song one after another from start to finish, because she didn't know that in a recording studio, you're allowed to play a song more than once, then mix and match the best parts. For the album, she won *Billboard* magazine's award for the best newcomer of the year. One of her most famous songs, "Universal Soldier," was included on the recording. The song protests against people fighting wars all over the world.

In only one short year, Buffy stopped playing to small crowds and was playing to huge audiences at famous concert halls in Canada, the United States and Mexico. She even performed at the famous Carnegie Hall in New York City. After her North American tour, she went on to perform in many Asian countries and Australia. Her songs were appreciated for their honesty and the way they tackled serious subjects, such as the unfair treatment of Aboriginal People.

But Buffy could not please everyone, and some thought she was a troublemaker with radical ideas that went against the US government. The 1960s was a decade when regular people questioned the government, especially in the United States. Because Buffy wasn't afraid to speak out, criticize injustice, and demand equality, she felt that her work was being held down, and that she didn't have the freedom of speech that was her right as an American citizen. Once, when she performed on the Tonight Show, one of the biggest late night talk shows on television, the producers told her that she wasn't allowed to play "Universal Soldier," "Now That the Buffalo's Gone," or any of her others songs that carried strong opinions.

In an article in *Maclean's* magazine, Buffy said that she wants her music to cross borders of time and to sing about things that matter to people everywhere. In her words, "the kinds of songs that would make as much sense in ancient Rome as they would today."

The attempts to keep Buffy down only made her stronger and more outspoken than ever.

Buffy Sainte-Marie

She is the kind of woman who won't stop at singing about injustice and hardship; she will think of ways to do something about it. The cause that was and is still closest to her is working for the rights of Aboriginal People, especially young people. Buffy remembered how lonely she sometimes felt as a child, isolated from her Cree heritage and in 1969, she started her own organization. It is called the Nihewan Foundation and is a

A studio portrait of Buffy in 1969.

non-profit group (a group that doesn't exist to make money). The word *nihewan* is from the Cree language and it means "be your culture." The foundation works to help educate young Aboriginals about their rich culture and to educate non-Aboriginals to understand traditional ways. It also supports Native children who have dreams of attending college or university.

Although Buffy's activism is obvious in her music, not every song she writes is meant to protest something. Another type of song that Buffy writes very well is the love song. One of her most famous is called "Until It's Time for You to Go." The song's success shows Buffy's ability to touch all different sorts of people with her music. Besides being recorded by many famous artists, such as Elvis Presley, Sonny and Cher, Barbra Streisand and Roberta Flack, the song was recorded by more than 200 other artists all over the world.

Buffy kept experimenting with her music and recorded an album with violins and other instruments, called *Endless Love*. Country music had always interested her, and in 1968 she traveled to Nashville, Tennessee, the country music capi-

tal of the United States, to record *I'm Gonna Be A Country Girl Again.*

In 1976, Buffy's life took a whole new direction. She started to make some big changes that affected her career for many years to come. She and her partner, Sheldon Wolfchild, moved to Kauai, Hawaii. They had a baby boy whom they named Dakota Starblanket Wolfchild (the name Starblanket comes from Buffy's mother's side of the family) or Cody for short. Buffy was happy to raise her son with love and support that she never got growing up, and she loved how eager Cody was to learn. Still influenced by her teaching background, Buffy decided to turn her attention away from adult music and try to reach the most important audience of all: children.

For the next five years, Buffy appeared regularly on the children's television program Sesame Street. Cameras came to visit Buffy's family in Hawaii. Along with Cody, Buffy taught young people across the country about their Aboriginal heritage and talked about different races of people living together in peace and with respect. She even taught one character, the Count, how to count to ten in Cree. Buffy also wrote a book for children, called *Nikosis and the Magic Hat,* and drew the pictures for the story.

Awards are one way to recognize and honor artists' achievements and in 1982, Buffy won an award that many people dream of: the Oscar. Her friend Jack Nitzsche was writing music for a Hollywood movie called *An Officer and A Gentleman* and he came to visit Buffy at her house in Hawaii. The two of them wrote a song together, "Up Where We Belong," for which Buffy's contribution was the melody, the main vocal part. Jack played the song for the director of the movie, who knew right away that he wanted it as the theme song for the film. The song, which was a duet, was recorded by Joe Cocker and Jennifer Warnes and earned Buffy the Oscar for Best Song from a Motion Picture.

It's hard to imagine a time before the Internet, but not so long ago it was still considered quite a new idea. It was not such a big part of people's lives and not as many people knew how to use it. In the early 1990s, Buffy recorded the album *Coincidence and Likely Stories*. Never one to be afraid of new things, Buffy proved that she was a pioneer in the music world. At home in Hawaii, she wrote and recorded all the songs on her computer and sent them to her record company in England over the Internet. At the time, the Internet was not used in this way and digital recordings were just starting to get popular. Buffy was one of the first to use the technology for her music.

Throughout her career, Buffy has worked to encourage Aboriginal People to reach their goals. Besides the Nihewan Foundation, Buffy has traveled to Native reserves across North America and the world to perform, to speak with local people, and to encourage them to believe in themselves. As an accomplished musician, Buffy affected the Canadian Juno Awards in a very important way. She helped start a new category of award, for Aboriginal Music in Canada, in 1992. She

> "In the '60s when everybody was joining Bob Dylan and Joan Baez in the antiwar marches, I was not there, because they didn't need me. I was on the reserves, where they did need me. Nobody was covering that base. So I would sacrifice fame for the true effectiveness of what I can do, where I can actually help. Getting your name in the paper is not what it's about. Sometimes shining the spotlight on local people, who cannot get their names in the paper, is what it's about."
> - Buffy Sainte-Marie in an interview with June Callwood

was inducted into the Juno Hall of Fame later that year.

Other than music, education is one of the things Buffy loves most, and she never stops learning. Not only does she have a PhD in Fine Arts from the University of Massachusetts, she also has degrees in teaching and philosophy. With such a high level of schooling, Buffy sometimes works as a professor teaching students about music, songwriting and Aboriginal culture at the University of Saskatchewan and York University.

Music is not the only art form Buffy uses to express herself. She also creates visual art with computers (digital art) that has been exhibited in museums in Calgary, Toronto, Vancouver, New York, Tuscon and Santa Fe. For her creations, she combines scanned pictures with different colors to represent the lives of Aboriginal People. Buffy describes her work as "painting with light."

Buffy has come a long way in her life. Having started on a small Aboriginal reserve in Saskatchewan, she is now a woman of the world. Not only has she explored many countries and learned from many different kinds of people, she is never afraid to let her creativity flow in the any direction. From the always-changing computer technology to traditional Aboriginal ways, Buffy welcomes what she doesn't know and strives to understand it. Best of all, she reaches out to others to let them know that they can do the same.

Joni Mitchell

1943 –

An artist can express herself in many different ways. It might be through music, painting, poetry, dance or by using other tools to create art that shows who she is and what she wants to say. Joni Mitchell is a true artist whose work comes in many forms. With her enormous talent and energy, Joni Mitchell has worked in lots of mediums (forms of art). Among all her artistic accomplishments, her songwriting and lyrics are probably the most powerful and have touched the most people, making Joni Mitchell one of the most important women in Canadian and American music.

Roberta Joan Anderson was born on November 7, 1943, in Fort MacLeod, Alberta. Her parents, Bill and Myrtle, noticed

that from an early age Joni had a creative streak, and they wanted to nurture it as much as possible. She loved to draw and paint, and was always considered to be the best artist in her class at school. She also loved music, so her parents enrolled her in piano lessons. The lessons weren't as fun as Joni thought they might be, because she had to play all the notes exactly as they were written. If she tried to change a song, her teacher would hit her on the knuckles with a ruler. Joni liked the classical pieces, but she wanted to play songs that she made up, such as "Robin Walk," which she wrote when she was seven. The teacher didn't understand why Joni would want to play her own songs, instead of playing the songs of the greatest composers who ever lived.

When Joni was nine her family moved to Saskatoon, Saskatchewan, the place she still calls her hometown. The same year, she got polio, a disease that can paralyze a person, and couldn't walk for several months. She promised herself that when she got better, she would spend her life creating music and art, and not waste a single day.

Joni did get better, and continued to practice. She was especially encouraged by her grade seven teacher, Arthur Kratzman, who could see that she was special. He taught Joni about another kind of art, using words instead of paint or music. Mr. Kratzman explained that an artist uses a brush and paint as tools to express ideas and creative feelings, and for a writer, words are her tools. Always wanting to explore new things, Joni opened up the toolbox in her head and started writing poetry.

As a teenager, Joni wanted to move on from the piano and learn the guitar, but she couldn't afford to buy one. Instead, she bought a secondhand ukulele and practiced on that. She started writing songs and performing at coffeehouses and at parties.

In 1963, Joni went to the Alberta College of Art, in Calgary, but only stayed one year. It felt like piano lessons all over again, where she couldn't express herself creatively. She made the big decision to move to Toronto and become a folksinger.

Joni Mitchell

Once in Toronto, Joni struggled to get by. She barely supported herself by working in department stores and couldn't get much work playing her music. During that difficult time, Joni also became

> "I wrote poetry, and I always wanted to make music. But I never put the two things together. Just a simple thing like being a singer-songwriter—that was a new idea. I realized that this was a whole new ballgame; now you could make your songs literature."
> - Joni Mitchell, from *Shadows and Light: Joni Mitchell, The Definitive Biography*

pregnant and gave birth to a baby girl in 1965. She tried to take care of her child, but decided an adoptive family could provide her daughter with more opportunities. It pained Joni to give her daughter up, but with no money, she didn't feel there was much choice.

Joni moved to Detroit and married folksinger Chuck Mitchell. Although they both had the same goals, the relationship did not last. After they broke up, Joni used her music to cope with her sadness, and threw herself into songwriting.

In 1967, Joni moved to New York City, which had a big music scene. She got a manager and started playing the folk music clubs. By the time she was 25 years old, she had written more than 60 songs. She began touring along the east coast of the United States, and her reputation grew so much that well-established singers like Buffy Sainte-Marie and Judy Collins asked to perform Joni's work. In 1969, she recorded the album *Clouds*, and was thrilled to finally be making enough money to support herself with her music. With her first big royalty cheque, Joni purchased a car which she named Bluebird.

Along with the group Crosby, Stills and Nash, Joni played at the Big Sur Folk Festival in California, performing in front of huge audiences of thousands of people in 1969. While it was a great opportunity, Joni preferred to play in places with small audiences, so she could feel connected to them. Her quiet, thought-

Joni in 1968, photographed with her guitar.

ful style didn't match the roar of the crowds and she sometimes found it hard to concentrate.

In 1970, Joni won a Grammy for Best Folk Performance and her new album, *Ladies of the Canyon*, went gold, selling 500,000 copies. Some of her most famous songs such as "Big Yellow Taxi" and "Woodstock" were on that album. She also performed a difficult show at the Isle of Wight Festival in England. The concert area was surrounded by tall wire fences and spectators felt hostile and restless. They threw things and some tried to get onstage. Joni was very nervous and asked the crowd to help her get through the set and to respect the other musicians. She managed to calm them down with her music.

After that incident, Joni decided she needed to take time off and get away. She had learned that being famous isn't necessarily the perfect life. Because she couldn't go out and do the same things as other people, she felt lonely and isolated by her fame. She traveled across Europe seeking inspiration and new things to sing about. She didn't just want to sing the same songs all the time.

Joni Mitchell

With all the new material she'd created, Joni released two more albums, *Blue* in 1971 and *For the Roses* in 1972. The peace she had found traveling was the ideal way for her to write songs. Everyone works best under certain conditions and for Joni, that meant being alone to write, so she could search deep down inside herself to find the music. All the soul-searching brought her to try different sounds and she moved away from folk music on her next album, *Court and Spark,* to play in the popular style. *Hejira* (which means to depart on a journey, a very appropriate title) was an album released in 1976 and was written while Joni drove across the United States by herself.

Fans continued to support Joni's music as its sound went further and further away from the folk music she started with. In 1975, Joni was the only woman to be nominated in the Album of the Year category at the Grammy Awards. She received three other nominations that same year.

The great jazz musician Charles Mingus asked Joni to write lyrics for a few songs he had come up with especially for her. She had always liked jazz music and wanted to collaborate with him, but wasn't sure how the project would turn out. Since most of Joni's creative projects started and ended with just her, building on someone else's idea was new to her, but she wanted to give it a shot. Charles, who was ill at the time and used a wheelchair, sometimes had difficulty expressing himself, but kept on working on the project with Joni, determined to make it work. They became friends and although Charles died before the album was completed, Joni made sure it was released in 1979 and titled it *Mingus.* Her collection of work was always growing and for that reason, she was inducted into the Canadian Music Hall of Fame in 1981.

Throughout her musical career, Joni always found time to keep up with her painting. While she was on the road in 1979, Joni worked up the courage to go and visit a painter she had always admired, Georgia O'Keeffe. The two women had painting

in common, but Georgia surprised Joni by revealing that at one time, she'd considered a career as a musician, which she had never pursued. Georgia thought it was best to do only one thing and to do it very well. Joni didn't agree with that idea; she was a songwriter and a painter and would never choose between the two. Painting was a big part of her life. She was very determined to keep it up and that same year her visual art was featured in a book of paintings called *StarArt*. Notes by Joni were also included, giving her impressions of each piece she had created.

In 1982, Joni married Larry Klein, a bass player and musical engineer who collaborated with her on the album *Wild Things Run Fast*. They complemented each other well, because of Joni's expertise with words and melodies, while Larry paid attention to rhythm and the details in a song. They went on a worldwide tour in 1983 that began in Osaka, Japan, and traveled through Australia and Europe. The schedule was exhausting and they would often find themselves in four different countries in as many days.

When she wasn't flying around the world playing concerts, one place Joni went to escape the craziness of touring was her house on the Sunshine Coast of Vancouver Island in British Columbia. She needed a sanctuary where she could concentrate on writing. In early September 1985, Joni found herself in the middle of a debate between other residents of the Coast and a salmon fishing company,

Joni has received many honors and awards throughout her career. In 1996 she was given the Governor General's Performing Arts Award; in 1997 she was inducted into the Songwriters Hall of Fame and was the first Canadian woman to be inducted into the Rock and Roll Hall of Fame; in 1995 she was presented with *Billboard* magazine's Century Award for distinguished creative achievement; in 2001, she received a star on Canada's Walk of Fame; in 2002 she received a Grammy Lifetime Achievement Award; and in 2004 she was made a Companion of the Order of Canada.

who wanted to use the land for their business. Joni's neighbors thought that a factory would ruin the natural beauty of the land and asked Joni to join in the protest. She did speak out against the fishing company, but was criticized by the media, who said she was just trying to show off what a big celebrity she was. It was hard to have negative things said about her, but she knew it was just a part of being famous. Over the years, Joni had grown very strong.

Despite all the wonderful career success Joni experienced, one of the greatest moments of her life had nothing to do with music. She never forgot about the baby girl she'd given up for adoption when she was 21, and she spent several years trying to find her, with no luck. Finally, in 1997, she was reunited with her daughter, Kilauren, who had also been searching for her birth mother. In the days leading up to their first meeting, all kinds of thoughts went through Joni's mind. She worried that Kilauren wouldn't like her, or that she would be angry that she had been given up for adoption. When mother and daughter

saw each other, they immediately felt a connection. Joni also found out that she was a grandmother to Kilauren's son Marlin.

It's not often that a popular musician is recognized not only by fans, but by serious scholars as well. Joni Mitchell's work was honored by the academic world in November 2004, when McGill University in Montreal held the Joni Mitchell Symposium. It was a day of lectures, discussions, and appreciation for Joni's career both in music and in art. She was also awarded with an honorary doctorate on the same day, because although Joni hadn't attended McGill, the university wanted to honor her for her life's accomplishments.

In her career, Joni has released over 20 albums, and after more than 35 years of making music, she continues to write and record. In her most recent album, *Songs of a Prairie Girl*, she has returned to her roots with a collection of songs related to growing up in Saskatchewan. Nothing can stop Joni Mitchell. She is a creative force, always searching for and finding inspiration in everything she does.

k.d. lang

1961 –

Small town life has the reputation for being quiet, not necessarily the kind of setting that springs to mind when you think of a world-famous singer. Consort, Alberta, is the small, friendly, prairie town where k.d. lang grew up. It has a grocery store and a gas station, but it's not a glamorous place, and probably not the kind of place you'd imagine as the hometown of someone who likes to stir up debate, and speak her mind even if others don't agree. She doesn't care how crazy she dances or how unpopular her ideas are; she just does what she feels is right for her. It just goes to show that a gutsy woman with exceptional talent can be found in an unlikely place.

Magnificent Women in Music

Katherine Dawn Lang was born on November 2, 1961. Her brother, John, and her two sisters, Jo Ann and Keltie, were all older than Kathy (the name she went by in her youth). Her mother was a teacher and her father owned a drugstore. One of her favorite games was pretending to be Batman. She had her first motorcycle by the time she was nine and could roller skate as fast as anyone in town. Life in the Lang household wasn't all that different from many other families and when Kathy's father left when she was 12, she helped her mother out with chores, scrubbing the bathtub and vacuuming.

As a teenager, Kathy was very athletic. Volleyball was her favorite sport, but she also played basketball and competed in track and field. She won competitions for javelin throwing. For three years in a row, Kathy was named Consort High School's Athlete of the Year.

Besides sports, Kathy loved music most of all. The piano was the first instrument she learned, but she had more fun playing the acoustic guitar, like the country and rock 'n' roll musicians on the radio. If Kathy's volleyball team took a bus trip to play in another town, she would lead the sing-along. She also sang at music festivals and usually won in her category. When she was 14 years old, she wrote her very first song, "Hoping My Dreams Come True."

Her interest in music took her to the college in Red Deer, Alberta, to study music and take voice lessons. Away from home for the first time, Kathy felt like she was on a whole new planet. She experimented with different styles of music, like jazz and punk rock, and became interested in theater. She became a vegetarian and learned about performance art. It was around this time that she changed her name, and started going by her initials, instead of Kathy. Also, she insisted on not using capital letters for her name, but only lower case letters, to make herself stand out from others.

k.d. lang

In 1982, k.d. starred in a musical called *Country Chorale*. The director of the play wanted k.d. to base her performance on the famous country singer, Patsy Cline. To prepare herself for the show, k.d. listened to Patsy's music and learned all the words by heart. Many of Patsy's songs were sweet and sad, and k.d. was inspired by the way Patsy used her voice to make people feel strong emotions. k.d. imagined herself singing in front of an audience, and decided to seriously pursue a career in music in hopes that one day people would enjoy listening to her as much as Patsy.

> Patsy Cline had a short but exceptional career as a country singer in the late 1950s and early 1960s. Her songs, such as "Walkin' After Midnight" and "Crazy" are now considered classics. Although she died in a plane crash when she was only 30 years old, she was awarded with a Grammy Lifetime Achievement Award, posthumously (after her death).

After the play ended, k.d. got a manager named Larry Wanagas, who helped her get work singing for radio commercials to earn money. On the side, she also formed a band called the Reclines, in honor of her favorite singer. k.d. didn't just sing well, she made sure she put on a show. Many woman country singers at the time wore pretty dresses and kept their hair long and loose. But k.d. was different. She kept her hair short, wore big puffy skirts, a plastic cowboy hat and boots, and horn-rim glasses. During the fast songs, she jumped up and down and encouraged the audience to have as much fun as she was.

k.d. released her first single in 1984, "Friday Dance Promenade." Her first album came out shortly after, called *A Truly Western Experience*. k.d. designed the cover. When the Reclines got to play the Edmonton Folk Festival, they had to perform in front of thousands of people; they'd never had such a big audience. k.d. sang her heart out and the concert ended with the crowd giving them a standing ovation. It was k.d.'s reputation for putting on such fun live shows that got Canadian college radio stations to start playing the Reclines. k.d. was known across the country as an up-and-coming musician and went on tour across the country in 1985.

It was a big year for k.d. Not only did she get to play at Expo '85 in Tsukuba, Japan, but after a show in a small club in New York City, she was offered a record deal with Sire Records— the same label that had signed Madonna and other successful acts. In November, k.d. won a Juno Award, the biggest music award in Canada, for Most Promising Female Vocalist. Always wanting to stand out from everyone else and show her quirky sense of humor, k.d. accepted the award wearing a big, white wedding dress. "I promise I'll continue to sing for all the right reasons," she said, imitating the promise a bride might make at her wedding.

> "You have to respect your audience…Without them, you're essentially standing alone, singing to yourself. That's not particularly appealing to an artist who craves the communal experience of sharing new ideas and sounds. The ideal scenario is to have an interactive give-and-take with your audience; to build and nurture a bond with them."
> - k.d. lang

The next album was called *Angel With A Lariat*, and although it sold fairly well, it wasn't the success k.d. was hoping for. The music industry wasn't sure what to make of k.d. or her music. She played mostly country, but her outrageous costumes and non-traditional style didn't fit into that category. She had the energy of a rock 'n' roll singer, but played twangy guitar on her songs. k.d. refused to be put into just one group and wouldn't change for anyone. Her individuality was something she would not compromise.

In 1987, k.d. became friends with famed musician Roy Orbison. He had succeeded at mixing the styles of rock and country, and appreciated k.d.'s talent and originality. He invited her to record a song with him, "Crying." It became one of k.d.'s

signature songs, and she won a Grammy Award for the duet in 1989.

Around this time k.d. decided to stop wearing the crazy country and western costumes. She toned down her outfits and began to perform in pants and suit jackets. Because it seemed that some people had difficulty seeing beyond her clothes she wanted to show the world that she was a serious musician. As her reputation as a talented singer grew, she began to perform in other sophisticated outfits, wearing long dresses and white gloves, or black pants and button-up shirts.

k.d. lang at a press conference during the Montreal World Film Festival in 1991.

k.d. continued to work hard at her music, and was rewarded for it. Her next record, *Shadowland*, earned her a Grammy Award for Best Female Country Vocalist. A fourth album, *Absolute Torch and Twang*, came out in 1989. She also began to speak out for causes she found important, as an activist. When she wasn't touring, k.d. performed at benefit concerts to support the fight against AIDS. In 1990, she worked to promote vegetarianism and to discourage people from eating animals. To match her outspoken personality, the slogan for k.d.'s campaign was "Meat Stinks." Some fans, especially in Alberta where there are many beef ranchers, angrily disagreed with her, and said they would stop buying her music. Some radio stations even refused to play

k.d. lang performing at a 2004 concert in Copenhagen, Denmark.

her albums. But k.d. was used to standing out, and wasn't influenced by the opinions of others.

We learn more and more about how important it is to accept people for who they are, and embrace differences. Sometimes it's not easy to just be yourself, instead of following the crowd. In 1992, when k.d. was being interviewed by a magazine called *The Advocate*, she admitted that she was a bit different from some celebrities, and came out as a lesbian. She was one of the first famous woman musicians to be open about that topic, and part of her was afraid that fans wouldn't accept it.

The success that followed only proved that she had nothing to fear. After four albums of country music, it was time to explore the different personalities of her music. She decided to take her sound in a new direction and experiment with different kinds of music, like jazz and pop. *Ingenue* (a word for someone who is very innocent and naïve, which k.d. certainly wasn't) had a sound that was much more mellow and melodic than her previous work. Instead of jumping around onstage to fast guitar strumming, k.d. sang standing mostly in one place, using all of her voice to communicate the emotion of the music to the audience. The album sold over one million copies and went platinum in the U.S., Australia, Britain and Canada.

Changing musical styles opened up many new opportunities for k.d. and she continued to put out records. She was also touring all the time, and started to feel tired and stressed. Outside of Vancouver, BC, she sometimes relaxed on the farm she shared with her sister, Keltie, but couldn't always find time to spend there and take care of the goats, pigs, dogs, and horses. It was time to move away to search for something different.

In Southern California, her new home, k.d. fell in love with the warm weather and the long streets lining the ocean. She could ride her motorcycle every day in the sunshine and felt rejuvenated by the sea air. Her lifestyle changed from hectic to much more easygoing and the beauty of her new surroundings inspired her to create the album, *Endless Summer*.

In 2002, k.d. felt ready to go back on the road after recording a duet with legendary jazz singer Tony Bennett. They went on a successful tour together during which k.d. indulged her love of jazz. Although she still lives in the United States, her latest album from 2004, *Hymns of the 49th Parallel*, is a tribute to some of the great singer-songwriters in Canada. The songs she chose were written by well-known Canadians like Jane Siberry, Leonard Cohen and Neil Young. Instead of the usual band made up of drums, guitar, bass and piano,

> In 1998, *Chatelaine* named k.d. lang Woman of the Year. The magazine often featured women who were considered attractive in a stylish way, who wore makeup and the latest fashions—something k.d. never did. Pleased that she got the title, k.d. said: "I'm not a stereotypical woman…I think it's great because they allowed me to be myself." She even wrote a song about it called "Miss Chatelaine."

k.d. went on a tour across North America with a symphony orchestra.

Over the years, k.d. has developed a spiritual outlook on life and converted to Buddhism, a religion that seeks inner peace and enlightenment. She takes her studies very seriously and works with a Tibetan Buddhist teacher. She still stands up for issues of gay rights and animal rights, and is still a vegetarian. She still loves to ride her motorcycle, and follows closely what's going on in the world of sports. Although she has never gone back to the outrageous costumes, she often performs concerts in bare feet, the way she feels most comfortable.

k.d. lang's journey has been full of twists and turns that led her to great success in the music world. Although talent, hard work, and bravery helped her become a world-famous singer, there is also one more element that kept her on the proper course: she was always true to herself and followed a path of her own choosing. Some people thought she was strange and others didn't understand her because she would not be put into just one narrow category. But her unique personality and style have gained her many fans who appreciate that she cannot be classified. While she's a bit country, a bit rock 'n' roll, a bit jazz and a bit pop, one knows for sure that she will always be completely k.d. lang.

CHANTAL KREVIAZUK

1973 –

It takes a strong person to take a difficult situation and turn it into something positive and inspiring. Although sometimes you may think it's easier to just give up, you know that when something bad happens, the right thing to do is face the challenge and just keep going. Chantal Kreviazuk is a woman who possesses the strength to do just this. In fact, when she found herself in the hospital after a serious accident—which would be frightening for a lot of people—she used the time to not only get well again, but to get her career started. Now she is one of Canada's great young musicians.

Chantal was born in Winnipeg, Manitoba, on May 18, 1973 to a family who was naturally musical. Their house was

Chantal performing at a wildfire relief benefit in Kamloops, BC.

rarely quiet. Chantal's grandparents, who immigrated to Canada from Ukraine, would tell her stories of the dances they attended when they were young. When she visited them, her grandmother played the harmonica, her grandfather played the fiddle and the rest of the family sang along.

When she was only three years old, Chantal begged her mother for piano lessons. She didn't think she was too young, but her mother wasn't so sure. The Kreviazuk boys, Michael and Trevor, always grumbled when it was time to practise; they didn't always feel like sitting at the bench and studying music. Mrs. Kreviazuk wondered whether Chantal was too little to take music seriously or whether she would get bored. She thought it would be best to wait a couple of years before starting her daughter on lessons.

So Chantal decided that just because she had to wait for lessons, it didn't mean that she had to wait to play. She sat at the piano, her legs still too short to reach the pedals, and pictured the songs she had seen her brothers play. Then she imagined the way the music sounded. Chantal began to learn how to play the piano all by herself, using what she called "hand-eye-ear coordination."

It didn't take long for everyone to see that the little girl had a big talent. Chantal loved the attention she would get from playing in front of people. At last, she was allowed to take music

Chantal Kreviazuk

lessons, and studied music and singing at the Royal Conservatory of Music. It takes a lot of dedication to learn an instrument, so Chantal's mother made sure to praise her daughter whenever she played something very well. But it wasn't all sheet music and practicing scales, Chantal could practice music by making a game out of it. Her mother would bet that she couldn't play a certain song that they had just heard on the radio (even though she never doubted her daughter could do it) and Chantal would sit at the piano and play it from start to finish, by ear. She didn't need to have the notes in front of her all the time.

Of course, Chantal took her piano lessons and playing music very seriously, but she couldn't shake a certain feeling in the back of her mind. She really enjoyed playing the classical pieces she learned, but they were all other people's songs. Chantal wanted to write and play her own songs.

As a teenager, Chantal actually started to make a bit of money doing what she loved. She wrote jingles for commercials and worked as a backup singer in music studios. Sometimes, she played lounge shows or at weddings. She enjoyed the work because she got to play music and it allowed her to always do something different. Chantal sometimes found it difficult to focus on one thing and was always on the move. Still, she continued to think about what it would be like to perform songs she had written and to sing lyrics that came from her heart.

Chantal continued her schooling at the University of Manitoba, where she took the Art Studies program and focused on classical piano. Her experience performing popular music and her classical training came together, and she began writing songs of her own, in secret. She didn't share them with anyone.

In 1994, Chantal went traveling in Europe, where every day brought something different, new and exciting. As it turned

> Chantal's name comes from the French word *chanter*, which means to sing.

out, it was not a typical holiday. It was in Italy that her life changed forever. One day, she rented a moped (a small motorized bicycle) to ride around and explore the Italian hills. It was a beautiful day, the kind where you think nothing can go wrong. But something did go wrong. During the trip, Chantal got into a head-on accident with a motorcycle. Her jaw was shattered, her leg was broken and she had to spend several painful months recovering in the hospital. She couldn't speak because she had pins in her jaw to help it heal. She couldn't walk or get into the bathtub without help, and at times felt frustrated and unhappy. Unable to go home to Canada until she got a bit better, Chantal was homesick. It would take many operations for her injuries to heal properly.

Spending so much time alone, with nothing to do but think, was difficult for someone who had always been on the move. Chantal thought about what was really important to her in life and what she could do to make every day count. Of course music had always been important, but it wasn't until she spent time in the hospital that she began to focus her creativity and to think seriously about a career. Instead of feeling sorry for herself, Chantal used the time in the hospital to get creative and write songs for her first album.

Sony Music signed Chantal to a record contract in 1996,

Chantal performing as part of a promotional tour in 2002 for *What If It All Means Something*.

when she was only 22 years old. It was a bit of a risk for the record company to sign someone so young that no one had heard of yet, but Chantal believed in herself and was determined to make the very best album she could. Many of the songs came from her own experiences, and it was a bit scary to share her private thoughts with the public. She

Lilith Fair is named after a biblical character. Although there is a lot of debate over the story, Lilith is said to have been created at the same time as Adam, the first man, to be his wife before Eve. But Lilith left the Garden of Eden because she didn't like taking orders from a man.

knew how lucky she was to get a record deal; she saw it as her chance to give something back for her good fortune by putting out the finest album possible. "I felt so blessed, but also like I owed people something," Chantal said.

When the album, called *Under These Rocks and Stones*, came out in 1997, Chantal discovered an audience of people who really appreciated her music, especially in Canada. That summer, she was invited to perform at Lilith Fair, a traveling music festival that was founded by Sarah McLachlan, a fellow Canadian singer/songwriter whom Chantal admired. Lilith Fair is the largest touring concert that features only women musicians.

Chantal's career was really taking off; her first album was out for everyone to hear and she got to play in front of big crowds at a popular festival. She began to gain a fan base and *Under These Rocks and Stones* sold over 100,000 copies. When Chantal recorded a version of a famous John Denver song, *Leaving On A Jet Plane*, which was used in the soundtrack of a Hollywood movie called *Armageddon*, she began to gain fans in the United States, too.

Her new life as a performer didn't stop her creativity. Her second album, called *Colour Moving and Still*, was released

shortly after the first, in 1999. Not only did she have a new album that year, but she also got married to Raine Maida, the lead singer for the rock band Our Lady Peace.

The Juno Awards, which were begun in 1970, are the biggest music award event in Canada; they celebrate both new and experienced Canadian musicians. When Chantal was nominated in the year 2000 for two categories, she couldn't believe it. It was an honor, not just because of the award, but mostly because of the pioneer women musicians who were nominated along with her, such as Joni Mitchell, Céline Dion and Alanis Morrisette. Rather than feel nervous, Chantal decided to be realistic when the big night came. She didn't think there was any way she could win against such accomplished musicians. Chantal decided to enjoy the evening as a spectator, not as a nominee. Because she pretended she wasn't nominated, Chantal got the shock of her life when she won for both the Best Pop/Adult Album of the year and for Best Female Artist.

Of course, she didn't let stardom or awards go to her head. Chantal has stayed focused on her songwriting, and knows that just because you win an award, it doesn't mean you can stop trying or stop putting your all into everything you do. "A Juno isn't going to write my next song for me," she says.

One thing that makes Chantal different from many other musicians is that she uses her fame to help those who are not as lucky as she is. One of her favorite charities is War Child, for which she has acted as a spokesperson. War Child works to raise money and awareness to help children affected by war all over the world. They put on concerts and sell CDs; the profits go to help promote children's rights and raise the quality of life for those living in countries where there is or has been war.

While Chantal has always donated a lot of her musical gift to charity, by playing concerts and recording songs for charity albums, in 2001 she felt she wanted to do something that went beyond music. That year, she and her husband traveled to Iraq to take part in a documentary film called *Musicians in the War Zone*. She visited a children's hospital where the doctors make only three dollars a week and patients needed medicine to get better but couldn't get it. What touched her most was meeting a group of little girls named Hanna, Ilauv, Noel and Fahtma. They were so young to have led such difficult lives and Chantal admired their bravery and the way they kept smiling. By the end of the trip, Chantal thought of the girls as her sisters.

With such a busy life, you'd think it would be hard for Chantal to be able to stay focused on her music. Between traveling and charity work, when would she find the time to write songs? One trick is that Chantal is *always* writing songs; she is inspired by real life and doesn't need to be in a certain place to concentrate. *What If It All Means Something*, her latest album, which was released in 2002, was written mostly while she was in motion, not standing still. Songs came to her while riding on an airplane, swimming at the beach, driving in a car or simply walking down the street. That record has been her most successful so far, and has sold over three million copies.

In 2003, Chantal made *Maclean's* magazine's Honour Roll, as one of the ten Canadians

> "I used to be concerned about everybody else—now I'm taking ownership of myself and my music and just letting it be. When you're true to yourself, the best comes out of you."
> - www.chantalonline.com

who made a difference because of her compassion for people. She also played a relief concert to benefit the victims of the 2004 Tsunami, and works with Zoocheck Canada, a group that works to make sure animals in zoos are treated humanely.

The role of mother was added to musician and humanitarian, when Chantal gave birth to her son, Rowan, in 2004 and in June of 2005 had a second son, Lucca Jon. Of course, Chantal continues to work on music, but not just her own. She enjoys collaborating with other recording artists to help them develop and grow the way she has. Such well-known singers as Avril Lavigne, Kelly Clarkson and Gwen Stefani all credit Chantal as a contributor on their newest albums.

Today, Chantal spends time in Toronto, Ontario and Malibu, California. She has learned to play the guitar and uses it along with the piano to write her beautiful melodies. Chantal is a musician who knows that fame is not the most important thing. What is important is how you use fame to communicate messages to others to help raise awareness for those who don't have a public voice. Although it took a serious accident to point Chantal in the right direction, she wouldn't take back any of the difficulties she has experienced. She is grateful for her musical talent and looks forward to many more years of hard work.

MEASHA BRUEGGERGOSMAN

1977 –

What do you think of when you hear the word "diva"? Do you think of someone with an incredible singing voice? Someone who wears lavish costumes? Someone who looks like she was born to perform for an audience, and does her best to be sure she deserves every bit of their applause? All of these ideas describe Measha Brueggergosman perfectly: a young diva who works hard to earn her place among the rising stars of classical music. Fans around the world can't wait to hear what great music she will make next.

Measha Gosman was born on the East Coast of Canada in Fredericton, New Brunswick, on June 28, 1977. Her family has deep roots in the community, and has lived there for five

generations. Measha loved growing up in a town that was not too big, and not too small, where there was a strong feeling of community. From the time she was young, her family encouraged her to work hard and told her she could accomplish whatever she wanted in life.

The Gosman children always got good grades in school, taking their studies seriously so they could go on to University. Measha studied hard too, and had many interests. Just like regular teenagers, she wanted to try many different things. When she wasn't singing, she was learning to play the trombone, playing rugby or running for a position on her school's student council. But something about her made her stand out from the rest of the crowd. While the other members of her family each had their own talents and all liked music, nobody's singing voice compared to the powerful soprano that came from Measha when she sang.

Every Sunday, Measha and her family attended the service at the local Baptist Church, and it was there that Measha was first able to practice singing at the top of her lungs. The congregation felt like a big family and everyone loved it when the girl with the amazing voice sang with the choir or belted out a gospel melody as a soloist. In church, Measha felt inspired. She decided that her talent was a gift from God that she must never take for granted, but rather share with as many people as she could reach.

In an interview with *The Globe and Mail*, Measha said that if she could have a slumber party and invite anyone she wanted, she would invite some of her favorite singers: Jann Arden, Holly Cole, Adrianne Pieczonka, Ella Fitzgerald and Tracy Dahl. All, except Ella, are Canadian singers.

Growing up, Measha always had a mischievous twinkle in her eye and a beautiful smile to match. Everyone in town hoped that she would go on to study music in a serious way. She even got a summer scholarship to the Boston Conserva-

tory to take voice lessons. The church and the community also supported Measha in another way, besides providing inspiration. When she graduated high school, she went on to study music full-time at the University of Toronto, but she returned to Fredericton every summer to give a concert, and all the money raised went towards paying for her university tuition.

Measha Brueggergosman at Roy Thomson Hall, Toronto.

One question people often ask Measha is where she got her unsual last name. They also want to know how to pronounce it correctly. Brueggergosman (BRU-gur-GOS-man) is actually an original name, which came about when Measha married Markus Bruegger, whom she met while he was attending her high school as an exchange student from Switzerland. The two of them decided that instead of following tradition—Measha changing her name or taking his name as well as hers, combined with a hyphen—they would combine both of their names and start a new tradition. Measha's unique, long last name goes well with her personal style of gorgeous, eye-catching costumes and commanding stage presence.

Once at university, Measha began working with voice teacher Mary Morrisson. She was only 18 years old when the lessons began, but Mary said she knew right away that she was helping to shape an extraordinary singer. As a music student, Measha's homework wasn't the same as her roommates, whose main assignments were to write essays and read hundreds of pages of textbooks. Measha's main homework, along with studying classical singing techniques and history, was to practice and learn to improve her voice. She spent most of her time practicing, working hard towards her goal of becoming a professional singer. If Measha wasn't home with her roommates, you could be sure she was doing vocal exercises and trying to master difficult pieces.

A small opera company called Queen of Puddings was casting classical singers for a new opera called *Beatrice Chancy*, and asked Mary if she knew any young female singers who would be good for the lead part. The libretto (or the words and story of the show) was written by the Canadian poet George Eliot Clarke and tells the story of a slave girl with an abusive father living in Nova Scotia in the 19th century. The person who played Beatrice would need a lot of passion, energy and emotion to fill such a demanding role.

At first, Mary suggested Measha for a smaller role because she was only 20 years old and didn't have much experience. But as soon as rehearsals started, the show's director gave her the lead part. They performed the opera in Halifax and Toronto to rave reviews. After seeing Measha's performance, one reporter wrote: "...every minute she is on stage you simply can't take your eyes off of her." The opera was filmed for CBC television, and Measha was nominated for a Gemini Award.

The early success did not make Measha decide to become a professional opera singer right away, because she knew she

"I always pray that people leave the performance changed, that in some small way, whatever they're going through—everybody's going through something—that it will at least be appeased or answers will be found or comfort will be given. That some kind of edification of the listener will take place. That's all I can do. That's really all I can do."
- Interview with Brad Wheeler, *The Globe and Mail*, December 17, 2004

had much more to learn about singing. Some advice she received (and took very seriously) was that if you want to grow as a person and as a singer, you should study at a variety of schools with a variety of teachers. That way, you are exposed to many styles and points of view. Measha also knew it would help her career to meet different people in the classical music world, learning as much as she could about style and technique.

After graduating from the University of Toronto with a bachelor's degree in music, Measha kept up her education. As a classical singer, she had to be able to sing in different languages, such as French, Italian and German. But to make the songs sound their best, she had to able to speak and understand the languages as well. Measha had the most trouble learning German, so she threw herself into a new challenge and moved to Germany to earn a master's degree in Duesseldorf, studying with Edith Wiens at the Robert Schumann Hochschule. A Canadian classically-trained singer with a huge international reputation, Edith was a great role model for Measha. After three years, she finished her degree and didn't stop there. She began working on her Meisterklassediplom, a German word for the studies you must complete just before beginning a PhD.

In 2002, Measha competed in the prestigious competition held by the Jeunesses Musicales International. The organization works to promote classical music to young people around the world and to reward young composers, singers and instrumentalists who have great talent. Measha performed at the event in Montreal and won the Grand

Not just a fan of music, but a fan of reading and literature, Measha participated in the 2004 panel for the CBC's Canada Reads. Every year, five Canadian celebrities are asked to choose their favorite Canadian book, and then talk about why they think their choice is the best. Measha chose *The Love of a Good Woman* by one of her favorite authors, Alice Munro.

Measha standing onstage at Roy Thomson Hall.

Prize that came with a bursary, which helped pay for her musical education.

When she begins to learn a new song, Measha studies it very carefully, just as she was taught in music school. She doesn't start off by singing it right away, in fact she doesn't sing the words until much later in the process. Before anything else, there is research to be done, so that she can learn the background of the song and understand the life of the composer. If the song is in a language other than English, Measha makes sure she understands every word, translating what she needs to translate so she knows exactly what the piece is supposed to communicate. Next, she studies the melody, to see how her vocals will fit in with the rest of the music. She is also careful to learn the rhythm of the song and she practices speaking the words in time to the beat, and then speaking them while playing along on the piano, so that everything is in perfect time.

Performing with an entire orchestra can be a daunting task for a singer, to make her voice the most powerful over all the other instruments, but Measha has done it many times in her career. Among the orchestras are those from cities such as Montreal, Vancouver, Quebec City, Baltimore, Boston, San Francisco and Berlin. Despite the excitement, Measha's true love is for giving recitals, where only she and a piano accompanist are on the stage. With only two different instruments—voice and piano—Measha feels closer to the audience, able to take them on a musical journey.

> "Being a Christian is something that I cling to in this profession…and once I came to terms with my identity…that I'm big, Black, and have massive amounts of hair, I was okay—once my self-esteem caught up with my physical presence."
> - Measha in an interview with *The Brunswickan*

Between performances, Measha tries to spend her time quietly, so she doesn't get too tired before the exhausting evening shows. If it's not time to practice, she tries to give her voice a chance to rest, and speaks as little as possible. She reads over her music, memorizing the lyrics to new songs. She drinks a lot of water to keep her throat from drying out and to keep her body's energy levels high. No matter how often she performs, at times she still feels nervous. But the best cure for nerves, according to Measha, is to be prepared so you have more confidence, knowing you're doing your best.

Measha has competed in singing competitions around the world and won an amazing number of awards for someone so young. In London, England, she won the Wigmore Hall International Song Competition in 2001; in Oslo, Norway, she won the Queen Sonja International Music Competition in 2003; and in Munich, Germany, she won the ARD Music Competition in

2003. Measha has also received grants (money to help her continue her singing) from the Canada Council and the Chalmers Fund. In 2004 Measha recorded and released her first album called *So Much to Tell.*

Visit Measha 's website at www. measha.com

As Measha has become famous, she has had the opportunity to perform for other famous people. Only the best performers are chosen to entertain royalty and when Measha was only 25 years old, she had the opportunity to sing for the Prince of Wales. She also felt honored to sing for Nelson Mandela, the South African freedom fighter.

Living the life of a performer takes Measha away from Canada for many months of the year. But even when she is far away, her family is never far from her thoughts. Although she has studied with some of the most accomplished teachers and met famous people, she says her parents are her biggest influence. She jokes that she did not inherit her musical ability from her parents, but what she did inherit from them was her strength. Measha's parents always taught her to be proud of herself and everything that makes her different and special. From her wild hair to her curvaceous figure, Measha is happy about who she is and what she has accomplished so far.

It takes a lot of confidence to get up on a stage and be the center of attention, but Measha is completely comfortable with herself and her talent. She wears bold, fantastic outfits onstage—bright pink shawls, flowing gowns, and sparkly makeup—her hair in a high crown above her head. And she usually performs in bare feet.

Sometimes, when she is exhausted by her busy traveling schedule, Measha remembers being back at the Baptist Church, where she first felt strength. Measha is a part of a new generation of divas, who are devoted to their singing, but never forget their beginnings, no matter how normal or humble. Surely, this is only the beginning of a great musical career.

VANESSA-MAE

1978-

When we first meet someone, we may try to pin them down based on where they come from, whether it's Canada, the United States, Kenya or Japan. When we talk about music, or first hear a song, we may do the same thing. We often try to classify it in terms of what genre (style) it belongs to, such as hip hop, rock 'n' roll, country, jazz, classical, or reggae. We each have our favorite genres, those we listen to most often and prefer over others. But there is some music that crosses boundaries and combines different genres, mixes lots of sounds together to really get our imaginations going. Vanessa-Mae is one woman you definitely can't pin down, who from birth was exposed to many different cultures. She creates music that is influenced

Magnificent Women in Music

by places all over the world. Just listen to one of her albums and you'll see there's almost nothing she can't do with her violin.

Vanessa-Mae Vanakorn Nicholson was born on October 27, 1978, in Singapore, which is an island in Southeast Asia. Its name comes from the Sanskrit words *singa* (lion) and *pura* (city). Vanessa's background is Chinese, on her mother Pamela's side, and Thai, on her father Vorapong's side. Her multicultural upbringing gave Vanessa an appreciation of different styles of music from a very young age. Because her parents divorced when she was only four years old, Vanessa didn't spend much time in the country of her birth, where she had already begun to take piano lessons. She and her mother moved together to London, England, shortly after the separation.

In London, Pamela remarried, and a British lawyer named Graham Nicholson became Vanessa's adopted father. As a hobby, he played the viola, which is a stringed instrument like the violin, but with a sound that is a bit lower. Graham thought it would be fun if Vanessa learned to play the violin, so they could practice together and play duets. At the age of five, when she picked up her first violin, Vanessa knew it was the instrument that she was meant to play.

Vanessa-Mae playing onstage at a concert.

Vanessa-Mae

She made the decision to stop her piano lessons so she could put all her energy into the violin. It wasn't because she wasn't good at both—she had even won a prize at a competition for the British Young Pianist of the Year—but the violin made her feel excited and energized, something the piano never did.

Pamela accepted her daughter's decision because she, too, felt that there was something special about Vanessa's violin playing. It wasn't just that she learned all the notes and scales quickly, but she was able to take very old songs and put a part of herself into them. It was almost as if the violin was a part of her body, she sounded so natural moving the bow across its strings. It didn't take long for Vanessa's violin teachers to notice too, and everyone was excited to discover that the young girl was more than just good: she was a prodigy, someone with an exceptional talent that inspires wonder in other people.

It became obvious that Vanessa needed the very best teachers to help develop her gift, so when she was eight years old she went to the Central Conservatoire in Beijing, China, to study with Professor Yin Lao Ji. Leaving home is not always easy, and Vanessa had to say goodbye to her family and friends to move to a country where nobody spoke English, the language she spoke at home. But any homesickness she felt at first went away after she got used to the new life. She learned Chinese and devoted herself to the lessons of the professor. Vanessa's days were filled with studying music, and she had to have a lot of self-discipline.

"Many things about me have changed, but something that will always remain is my determination to play music that satisfies me, and never to be restricted by categories imposed arbitrarily from outside. I have continued to play, and will always love, classical music—it is my heritage. But I will always want to experiment, to discover new musical experiences. This is just the beginning, I can promise you!"
- Vanessa-Mae, EMI Press release 2002

Magnificent Women in Music

The classical way of playing that she learned was the Yan-kelevich Technique, which teaches the violin player to put all her body's energy into the music while she plays.

Most students who followed the same course in Beijing as Vanessa took three years to complete it. Vanessa, however, finished in only a few months, and what made this an even greater achievement was the fact that she was Professor Lao Ji's youngest student; most of the other students were thirteen or older. Vanessa then returned to England an even better musician than before. Next, she studied at the Royal College of Music with one of the top violin teachers from Russia, named Felix Andrievsky. The youngest person ever to be enrolled in the College, Vanessa graduated from the same courses as people in their teens or early adult years. Later, Felix said how much he admired the young girl and that it almost made him jealous that she could play the most complicated pieces as though they were easy.

The first time Vanessa performed in front of a large audience of music lovers was with the London Philharmonic Orchestra. She caused a sensation, not only because of her expert playing, but because she was just ten years old at the time. Her first tour was with the London Mozart Players (named after the famous Austrian composer) and her first CD was released in 1991, a few months before her twelfth birthday. By the time she was 13, Vanessa had recorded three albums. On the third, she played the concertos (music during which a solo musician is accompanied by an orchestra) of Tchaikovsky and Beethoven, and once again she was the youngest person ever to record those particular pieces.

In order to achieve the right sound for a song, the type of instrument is very important. Different violins each have their own special strengths. Vanessa's main violin is a Guadagnini acoustic violin with a wooden body and a traditional sound. It was made in Italy in the year 1761 and Vanessa nicknamed it Gizmo. In 1992, Vanessa began using a very special violin that would help change the way she played. An electric violin by the company Zeta, it is different from the traditional violins she usually played. Its body is smaller than most, shaped differently and the sound is more aggressive. It occurred to Vanessa that instead of always playing the delicate classical pieces, she could add some strong beats to make it sound more like the popular music played on the radio. Vanessa didn't understand why music could only be played a certain way, and why music of different styles and cultures couldn't work together, just as people of different styles and cultures do. She decided to try to bring together, or fuse, two different styles of music and create something brand new.

What came out of this idea was Vanessa's 1995 album, *The Violin Player.* It was a blend of classical songs and popular dance music. It was a huge risk for Vanessa to follow her own path and experiment with traditional music. Even though she was still a teenager, her career as a classical violinist was already solid. She had fans all over the world who enjoyed her playing familiar music in the familiar way. But just as she knew when she was only five that she should give up piano and concentrate on violin, again she knew she had to make her own music.

Some people who had very set ideas about what classical music should sound like and how it should be played did not like Vanessa's new style of music. They thought it was wrong to change songs that had so much tradition around them. But even those who were critical of Vanessa still gave her credit for her skills; there was no debate over the fact that no matter what the music, Vanessa's talent outshone everyone else's. It turned out that Vanessa did not lose fans over changing her music; she gained fans. "Toccata & Fugue" was the first single released off the new record. It went to the top of the music charts in England, making Vanessa the very first classical artist to cross over and have a hit song on the dance charts. *The Violin Player* sold millions of copies.

Over the next few years, Vanessa worked on her music constantly. She didn't just focus on one style of music, but kept up with classical, fusion and even traditional Chinese music,

which she explored in honor of her mother's side of the family. *The Classical Album*, *China Girl* and *Storm* were all very different albums. Her popularity began to catch on in North America, as well as Europe and Asia, and she was on *People* magazine's list of the 50 most beautiful celebrities in 1996. Vanessa also won many international awards. She is the only instrumental musician to win Best Female Artist at the BRIT Awards. She also received the HMV Silver Clef Award for the top international artist of the year.

Vanessa had so much success before she was even 18 years old, it was hard to imagine things would get even better. A great moment in her career occurred in 1997 when she was the only non-native of China asked to perform at the reunification ceremony in Hong Kong. Up until that time, Hong Kong had been a British colony, but in the summer of that year it became part of China again. This was a huge honor for Vanessa, because the event was a celebration of Chinese unity, and even though she is of mixed background and not born in China, the Chinese accepted her as one of their own, and welcomed her participation in the historic celebration.

To reach different audiences with her music, Vanessa has journeyed around the world many times. She has given concerts in over 50 countries and played at some of the most exciting places, such as Moscow's Kremlin Palace, the Acropolis in Athens, Times Square in New York City, and Buckingham Palace.

Imagine standing at the top of a mountain, looking down at a huge crowd of people who look like tiny insects because you are so high up. That would be enough to make even the

Vanessa-Mae

bravest person a bit nervous, but next, imagine that you take a running start and soar down to the audience on a hang-glider, land on a stage and launch into performing a concert. For many performers, it is hard to deal with the fear of just walking onto the stage. But Vanessa's adventurous spirit makes her push past the limits of what others will do. She wants to make her concerts as fun and exciting as possible for every person watching. Entering on a hang glider is exactly what she did in St. Moritz, Switzerland, to begin her performance in a concert held on a frozen lake. She wore a

An intriguing fact about Vanessa is that she has the same birthday as Niccolò Paganini, the great Italian composer and violinist, and one of the first superstars of the violin world. Although he was born in the year 1782, almost two hundred years before Vanessa, fans like to imagine that this coincidence has somehow helped her. Paganini was a naturally exciting performer who was full of energy, and some fans of violin music feel the spirit of the 18th century musician is similar to Vanessa's style.

helmet and special suit for safety, but as soon as she landed, she unzipped the suit to reveal a gorgeous costume underneath, perfectly suited to the lively performance she gave that night.

Magnificent Women in Music

Vanessa always challenges herself and her musical talents, never content to stick with just one style, or play for just one type of audience. For her 2001 album called *Subject to Change*, Vanessa collaborated with British dance music producer Youth, to keep experimenting with dance and classical fusion. She has worked on many projects with popular performers, like Janet Jackson and Prince, and some of her music was included on the soundtrack to the animated Disney movie *Mulan*. Her latest album, *Choreography*, is a mixture of beats and rhythms from all over the world, drawn from her travel experience. Songs are based on the tango from Argentina, the bolero from Spain, the music of India and traditional African tribal dances.

Through all the touring and hard work, Vanessa has not forgotten to spend time on other things that are important to her. She volunteers for the Red Cross and through them she has traveled to Kenya and Cambodia. She also gives many charity performances to benefit that organization. Vanessa is very close to her mother, Pamela, who managed her career until 2002. In the early days of Vanessa's career, Pamela accompanied her on the piano during performances.

Vanessa-Mae had the good luck to start life with many different cultural influences: her parents' cultures of Thailand and China, her move to England and then her studies in China were just the beginning of the exposure she would get to the world's diverse people and places when she traveled later on. She brings this diversity to her music and has fans from different countries all over the world, who appreciate her combining tradition and innovation to give audiences a whole new musical experience. In her career, which is not yet 20 years long, she has released more than a dozen albums and shows no sign of slowing down. A musical pioneer who continues to change and grow with every project, it's impossible to guess what Vanessa will do next, but it is fun to imagine the limitless possibilities.

RESOURCES

Places to look for more women musicians:

Bowers, Jane and Judith Tick, editors. *Women Making Music: The Western Art Tradition, 1150-1950.* Urbana : University of Illinois Press, 1986.

Hixon, Donald L. *Women in Music : an Encyclopedic Biobibliography.* Lanham, MD: Scarecrow Press, 1993.

Pendle, Karin, editor. *Women & Music : a History.* Bloomington, IN: Indiana University Press, 2000.

www.iawm.com (International Alliance for Women in Music) resources link

www.womensmusic.com

www.womenofnote.co.uk

Try Google or your library for these women:

Amy Beach, Hildegard von Bingen, Nadia Boulanger, Montserrat Caballé, Francesca Caccini, Maria Callas, Cecile Chaminade, Jean Coulthard, Ruth Crawford-Seeger, Jacqueline du Pré, Sophie Eckhardt-Gramatté, Teodora Ginés, Sofia Gubaidulina, Fanny Mendelssohn Hensel, Wanda Landowska, Jenny Lind, Melba Liston, Myriam Makeba, Erica Morini, Thea Musgrave, Maria Theresia von Paradis, Beverly Sills, Barbara Strozzi, Joan Sutherland, Renata Tebaldi, Joan Tower, Pauline Viardot-Garcia

Magnificent Women in Music

Clara Wieck Schumann

Reich, Nancy. *Clara Schumann: The Artist and the Woman.*
Ithaca: Cornell University Press, 1986.

Reich, Susanna. *Clara Schumann: Piano Virtuoso.* New York:
Clarion Books, 1999.

The Clara Schumann Society
www.claraschumann.net

Clara Schumann brief biography by Carol Traxler
www.geocities.com/Vienna/Strasse/1945/WSB/clara.html

Chronology of Clara Schumann
www.scils.rutgers.edu/~eversr/biograph.html

Dame Ethel Smyth

Bowers, Jane and Judith Tick (editors). *Women Making Music.*
Chicago: University of Illinois Press, 1987.

Nichols, Janet. *Women Music Makers: An Introduction to Women
Composers.* New York. Walker and Company, 1992.

St. John, Christopher. *Ethel Smyth: A Biography.* London:
Longmans, 1959.

www.ibiblio.org/cheryb/women/dame-ethel.html

www.classical-composers.org/cgi-bin/ccd.cgi?comp=smyth

www.sandscapepublications.com/intouch/ethelsmyth.html

Marian Anderson

Ferris, Jeri. *What I Had Was Singing: The Story of Marian Anderson.* Minneapolis: Carolrhoda Books, Inc. 1994.

Tedards, Anne. *Marian Anderson: Singer.* New York: Chelsea House Publishers, 1988.

Marian Anderson: The Story of the Voice that Broke Barriers. Greater Washington Educational Telecommunica tions Association, 1991. (video)

Women in History: Living Vignettes of Notable Women from U.S. History http://www.lkwdpl.org/wihohio/ande-mar. htm

University of Pennsylvania Rare Book and Manuscript Library: Marian Anderson http://www.library.upenn.edu/ collections/rbm/photos/manderson.html

Ella Fitzgerald

Ella Fitzgerald: Official Web Site www.ellafitzgerald.com

Haskins, Jim. *Ella Fitzgerald: A Life Through Jazz.* Kent, United Kingdom: New English Library, 1991.

Rennet, Richard. *Profiles of Great Black Americans: Jazz Stars.* New York: Chelsea House Publishers, 1994.

Ella Fitzgerald: Forever Ella. A&E Television Network Biography, 2000. (video)

Buffy Sainte-Marie

Callwood, June. *June Callwood's National Treasures*. Toronto: Stoddart Publishing Co. Limited, 1994.

Wright-McLeod, Brian. "Sainte-Marie's 24th album shows passion, care and simple honesty." *Wind Speaker*. March 1996.

"Buffy Sainte-Marie: singer." *Contemporary Canadian Musicians,* September 1998.

"Buffy Sainte-Marie." *People Weekly,* June 17, 1996 v45 n24.

www.buffysaintemarie.co.uk

Buffy Sainte-Marie's website
www.creative-native.com

Buffy Sainte-Marie's Nihewan Foundation
www.nihewan.org

www.northernstars.ca

Joni Mitchell

Adria, Marco. *Music of Our Times: Eight Canadian Singer-Song-writers*. Toronto: James Lorimer and Company, 1990.

Hinton, Brian. *Joni Mitchell: Both Sides Now*. London: Sanctuary Publishing Limited, 1996.

O'Brien, Karen. *Shadows and Light: Joni Mitchell, the Definitive Biography*. London: Virgin Books, 2001.

Joni Mitchell Official Website
www.jonimitchell.com

A Woman of Heart and Mind: The Life and Times of Joni Mitchell www.cbc.ca/lifeandtimes/mitchell.html

www.heroines.ca/people/mitchell.html

Joni Mitchell Symposium, McGill University
www.mcgill.ca/music/events/jmitchell_symposium/

www.artistdirect.com/nad/music/artist/bio/0,,468974,00.html#bio

k.d. lang

Adria, Marco. *Music of Our Times: Eight Canadian Singer-Songwriters.* Toronto: James Lorimer & Company Limited, 1990.

Martinac, Paula. *k.d. lang.* Philadelphia: Chelsea House Publishers, 1995.

Robertson, William. *k.d. lang: Carrying the Torch.* Toronto: ECW Press, 1992.

Official website of k.d. lang
www.kdlang.com

Warner Bros. Records Inc.
www.wbr.com/kdlang/biography.html

Online biography
www.mp3.com/k.d.-lang/artists/77652/biography.html

Magnificent Women in Music

Measha Brueggergosman

Batt, Maureen. "Not Just Your Average Superstar." *The Brunswickan*. March 30, 2005.

Caldwell, Rebecca. "Artist's Life: Measha Bruggergosman." *The Globe and Mail*. August 4, 2001.

Eatock, Colin. "Hitting the High Notes from Fredericton." *The Globe and Mail*. February 12, 2000.

Everett-Green, Robert. "Measha factor: ever the diva, this young soprano is taking fame in stride." *The Globe and Mail*. October 26, 2002.

Wolfe, Helen. *A Woman's Agenda 2003: Celebrating Movers and Shakers*. Toronto: Second Story Press, 2003.

Encyclopedia of Music in Canada
www.thecanadianencyclopedia.com

Measha Brueggergosman's Website
www.measha.com

Chantal Kreviazuk

www.absolutedivas.com/chantal/biography.shtml

www.canehdian.com/artistlinks/chantalkreviazuk/biography.html

www.chantal-k.com/

www.chantalonline.com (Official website of Chantal Kreviazuk)

www.concertlivewire.com/interviews/chantal.htm

www.geocities.com/chantal_fan/afh-biography.html

www.rockpublication.com/chantalkreviazuk.htm

www.socan.ca/jsp/en/news_events/feature_stories/Chantal.
jsp

www.warchild.ca

Vanessa-Mae
The Red Hot Vanessa-Mae Homepage
www.vanessamae.com

Vanessa-Mae Official Website of Sony Music
www.vanessa-mae.com

The Four Seasons of Vanessa-Mae Website
www.vanessamae.org

The Magic of Vanessa-Mae Website
http://vanessa-mae.org/

Photo Credits

Front cover
Chantal Kreviazuk: photo by PictureChasers.com
Joni Mitchell: Prazak, Frank/Library and Archives Canada/PA-211916
Vanessa-Mae: photo by Pierre-Michel Virot
Marian Anderson: Library of Congress, Prints & Photographs Division, Carl Van Vechten Collection, LC-USZ62-114554
Measha Brueggergosman: photo by Lorne Bridgman

Clara Schumann
Page 11: Robert-Schumann-Haus Zwickau; Archiv-Nr.: 10054 - B2
Page 12: Robert-Schumann-Haus Zwickau; Archiv-Nr.: 10462 - B2
Page 16: Robert-Schumann-Haus Zwickau; Archiv-Nr.: 10059 - B2

Dame Ethel Smyth
Page 21: National Portrait Gallery, London

Marian Anderson
Page 29: Library of Congress, Prints & Photographs Division, Carl Van Vechten Collection, LC-USZ62-114554
Page 34: Library of Congress, Prints & Photographs Division, Carl Van Vechten Collection, LC-USZ62-103734

Ella Fitzgerald
Page 39: Library of Congress, Prints & Photographs Division, Carl Van Vechten Collection, LC-USZ62-100859
Page 42: Library of Congress, Prints & Photographs Division, Carl Van Vechten Collection, LC-USZ62-118965

Magnificent Women in Music

Buffy Sainte-Marie
All photos by Jack Robinson.

Joni Mitchell
Page 57: photo by Jack Robinson
Page 60: Prazak, Frank/Library and Archives Canada/PA-211916
Page 63: photo by Jack Robinson

k.d. lang
Page 65: photo by Lois Siegel
Page 69: photo by Lois Siegel
Page 70: photo by Martin Rosenauer

Chantal Kreviazuk
Page 73: photo by PictureChasers.com
Page 74: photo by PictureChasers.com
Page 76: photo by Terence Gui
Page 78: photo by Terence Gui

Meahsa Brueggergosman
Photos courtesy Lorne Bridgman. All photos taken at Roy Thomson Hall, Toronto.

Vanessa-Mae
All photos by Pierre-Michel Virot.